Pembina Country

Paul Jones

Caitlin
Press

Caitlin Press Inc.
Box 2387, Stn. B
Prince George, BC
V2N 2S6

Cover design by Eye Design Inc.
Index by Kathy Plett.
Page design and output by David Lee Communications.

Caitlin Press acknowledges the support of the Canada Council for the Arts for our publishing program. Similarly, we acknowledge the support of the Arts Council of British Columbia.

THE CANADA COUNCIL | LE CONSEIL DES ARTS
FOR THE ARTS | DU CANADA
SINCE 1957 | DEPUIS 1957

Canadian Cataloguing in Publication Data

Jones, Paul, 1921–
    Pembina country

ISBN 0-920576-73-7

1. Jones, Paul, 1921– 2. Frontier and pioneer life—Alberta—Pembina River Region. 3. Pembina River Region (Alta.)—Biography. I. Title.
FC3695.P45Z49 1998   971.23'3   C98-910252-1
F1079.P45J66 1998

Contents

For
Ryan,
Dayna
& Jacob

Foreword

IT WAS MY TIME, AND THE TIME OF MY GENERATION. IT WASN'T A good time, but then, we didn't choose it: we were born into it.

This book is not about the Great Depression—others have written eloquently and copiously on that subject—but it is about how we lived during those depressed years and how we, the children of the nineteen-twenties and thirties, had our lives shaped by them.

Undoubtedly things would have been easier had money been more plentiful when we were growing up, but much of what happened would have happened anyway. People being products of their roots and upbringing, their behavioural characteristics do not vary markedly over the long haul. Regardless of economics, they succeed or fail, one way or another, despite wealth or the lack of it. My parents would have failed because they were the kind of people who were born to fail. In saying this, I mean no disloyalty or disrespect. They were good people and they tried. They harmed nobody but themselves and they recognized that their misfortunes were to a great extent of their own making.

That they would fail was inevitable, but along the way, they instilled in my sister, my brother and me a set of values—based on the Ten Commandments from the one side, and army discipline from the other—that would govern the rest of our lives. They also instilled in us a determination to rise above what they, as class-conscious Britons, conceived to be our station in life. In these endeavours, at least, they achieved a measure of success.

They were transplanted to middle Alberta from the United Kingdom, largely by chance, the result of happenings over which they had no control. Unlike hundreds of other couples in the post First-World-War years, theirs was not a planned migration to a land of greater opportunity where they hoped to better themselves. They came because there was little alternative.

Theirs was a curious union. Products of different backgrounds, they came together, not through mutual interests or like lifestyles, but because of a common responsibility that was thrust upon them.

As a family we were not unique. There were dozens like us, scattered throughout the Alberta bushland. We lived from one day to the next with little to look forward to. And for children in their formative years, there was not much of the stuff from which to fashion dreams of the future. That so many succeeded and even prospered is indeed remarkable.

I was born eight years before the crash of '29 that is credited with kicking off the depression years. These stories are windows on the life of an unspectacular family and particularly on me, the eldest son. They span the period from 1886 when my father was born to the present, when after more than half a century, I returned to the place of my birth, the farming community of Sangudo, Alberta.

My Dream

I dreamed I saw the place of my boyhood.
In summer rain I saw it.
I saw the oat fields flattened waves
and the poplar leaves blown silver.
I saw the tall hay grasses bend
and I felt the warm prairie wind.
I smelled sweet clover and strawberry vine.
and I smelled saddle leather and wet cattle.
I heard meadowlarks and the sound of trickling water.
and I felt the blue clay tug at my feet

In my dream I heard the sound of wagons,
and I heard trace chains jingle.
I saw the roadway, tracked with horses and iron wheels
and, bright in the gloom, I saw the blacksmith's forge,
and stars, showering from white hot metal
shattered on the singing anvil.
I smelled wood smoke, horse sweat
and the pungency of manure.

I saw grain elevators tall against the sky
and beside them, rattling freight trains,
passing on shining rails.
I felt the soft earth tremble with their going
and I heard their clatter.
I heard boot heels drumming on wooden sidewalks,
the slam of screen doors
and, sounding above the whispering rain,
long forgotten voices.

Paul Jones

I saw a small cottage with a crooked chimney,
its grey shingles shining in the rain.
and a garden with green cabbage
and long straight rows of potatoes.
I heard the song of the piano in the late afternoon
and I smelled the smell of fresh baked bread.

And I wept for my home in the rain.
I wept for the derelict schoolhouse,
the doors boarded over. The cemetery,
weed grown and the tombstones toppled,
the names of those I once loved
lying obscure, under dark leaves and creeping moss.
I heard lonely sighing through broken window panes
and the sound of windblown shutters, creaking.
I smelled decay, and in my dream I wept.

—Paul Jones

1 • *Pembina Country Revisited*

THE ROAD IS A THIN WEDGE POINTING DUE NORTH FROM THE highway. It is straighter now. It still undulates and slices through muskeg where the black spruce and tamarack stand with bowed heads; that much, at least, hasn't changed. Back at the junction, where we turned off Highway 16, the green sign said "757 Sangudo 31 kilometres." As I remember, the road wasn't numbered. None of the roads were. There was no paving either. It was a wagon track, rutted and winding between the sloughs, pure grease when wet, hard as concrete when dry.

A few kilometres further along, a sign on a white post points east and says "Stanger." There is no collection of buildings that would indicate a village. There never was much there. Like Orangeville and Padstow, Stanger was the name of a school and a post office, nothing more. I think the school is probably gone, the children bussed to a larger centre, and the post office will have closed. Canada Post, in its fanatical drive for efficiency, will have long ago seen to that. Now, I guess, all that is left of Stanger is the sign on the white post.

I keep the speedometer standing at a hundred kilometres and watch the country slide by. At that speed, my memory can't unravel it quickly enough. I can't get the contours sorted out before we are on to the next ones. Even fifty kilometres an hour was unheard of the last time I passed this way. The distance is compressed by the speed. What once seemed such a long way is but a moment, now. I feel I should slow down and examine it mile by mile, hill by hill, but there is no time. We have allocated only two days to looking into the past. We must get on with it.

The sky is the same, a deep cobalt blue, its dome supporting white, scimitar-shaped clouds. It is a sky of late summer. Nothing of significance reaches up from the horizon to intrude into it. Here the land is round and gentle, tufted with short poplars and willows between the muskeg and yellow fields. There are no great landmarks. We left the foothills of the Rocky Mountains back at Hinton.

We come to the railroad at a level crossing. The road has always crossed the track here and then turned left to parallel it. Now 757 continues straight on, bypassing the town, but the old road is still there. I turn onto it. It is pretty much the same as I remember except it is paved. We arrive at the outskirts of town where the outskirts always were. The town, obviously, hasn't grown in this direction. The grain elevators are still the only structures of importance. There used to be only one, painted red. Now there are two, and they are green, the colour of the countryside. The railroad water tank and the station buildings are gone. I guess the train doesn't stop here anymore.

Above on the hill, to the right of the United church spire, is the old school house. It looks dilapidated. I see that the windows, through which I watched steam locomotives shunt boxcars on the siding instead of paying attention to Miss Penny, are boarded over. There must be a more modern school somewhere. I drive slowly up the hill where once we rode our sleds at breakneck speeds on winter evenings. I search the houses along the sides and recognize a few. The names of those who dwelt in them come back to me.

The livery barn is gone, along with the loungers who chewed straws in the doorway, and gone are the clouds of sparrows that eked out a living on the undigested seeds in the brown horse manure littering the road in front of it.

The hotel is still there, though, a dull, grey, uninviting box of a building with blank windows and two dark doors. One of which always stood open on warm summer evenings, and through which raucous sounds and sometimes the instigators of beery arguments were expelled noisily into the night. If it was necessary to find Father, it was the first place to look. We round the corner, and arrive on the main street. I angle park in the middle of a block. I see that the street is still only two blocks long.

I am home at last.

I'm not sure what has brought me back here. When we moved away in 1938, we left nothing behind. We relinquished any claim to the land on which we lived. We left no family and few real friends. The blue clay of the cemetery does not hold the bones of any ancestor. All I have is a memory of a time, one that can't be shared with a family member, since I am the last of them. For the past year I have felt compelled to revisit this place where I and my brother and sister had our beginnings, and where our parents struggled and failed to carve a sustaining livelihood from the raw bushland. I have felt the need to see it again, to reconcile memory with reality. How much of what I remember is real. How much is imagination. I will find out.

"This is it then," my wife says. "This is Sangudo."

"This is it," I reply.

"What do you want to do first?"

"I don't know, but I guess I better find someone who knows where things are. Maybe I can get a map. I know where I am in town, but I'm sure the countryside has changed. What were small homesteads are now probably huge farms."

"It's only two o'clock. We have time. Why don't you see if you can find your old home first? We can look around town tomorrow.

"What about a place to stay?" I ask.

"Don't worry about it. We'll find something later."

13

I say, "The hotel was never very good, and it doesn't look like it has improved. There must be a motel or something, though." Over my shoulder I see a sign that says 'Village Office.' "They must know something in there. I'll only be a moment. I'll see what I can find out."

The pleasant-looking young woman in the office is smiling and talking into the telephone. She takes it from her ear and buries it in her bosom.

"Can I help you?" she asks with a look that tells me I'm interrupting.

"Go ahead with your call," I say.

"This may take awhile. I'm talking to my husband."

"I might take a while too, so go ahead. I can wait."

She hurries her call; I can tell.

"Now, what can I do for you?" she asks, hanging up.

Suddenly, I am at a loss to describe what I am looking for. I blurt out that I am here after fifty-six years, looking for things, people and places that I might remember and, although I didn't say so, I guess I am looking for someone who might remember me. She is nice about it. She is pretty much a newcomer to the community, but she knows some of the old-timers. I deal out a few names, and she is able to connect with some of them. Most of all, I am looking for directions to our old homestead. I know the roads have changed and I'm not sure I can find it. With this she can't help me; she doesn't know the country well enough.

She gives me a historical brochure, fifty years of Sangudo, 1937 to 1987. On it is a picture taken in 1937. I recognize every building, but it doesn't point the way to the homestead.

"Why don't you go to the county office?" she says. "They have all the maps. I'm sure they can help you." She tells me where it is. I thank her and walk a few doors down the street. I study the buildings. Some are old. I try to figure out who occupied them. I recognize one that was a grocery store. I know because I helped to build it. I carried river stones in a bucket and pushed them down into the fresh cement as it was poured into the foundation forms. As I walk, I get a feeling that I am an alien, someone from another time warp. I know all about this town, exactly where I am and where everything used to be, but nobody knows me.

In the county office, another pleasant woman asks if she can help me. I tell her what I want. Fortunately, I know the legal description of the property. Sometimes I can't remember what I had for breakfast, but that legal description has hung in my mind since I was six years old and Father deciphered the strange marks on the iron pin at the corner of our field into something meaningful: N.E. Quarter of Section 16, Township 56, Range 7, West of the 5th meridian. She finds the parcel on a huge map pinned to the wall. Another woman comes in and between the three of us we figure out the roads to get there.

"Well, do you know where to go?" my wife asks, as I get back in the car.

"I think so. If I can get started right and remember everything they told me."

We drive out the north end of town and find the bridge over the Pembina River. It's not where I remember it. At some time, it has been moved upstream, closer to town. It is of a modern design, sleek and clean, without extraneous truss-work, and it is high above the water. It doesn't have much character. It's not like the heavy-timbered cantilevered old one, the one we used to crawl around on—as a change from crawling on the railroad bridge. The old bridge was more fun for young boys.

I remember the spring when the river exerted its muscle and swept that bridge aside as though it was made of straw. After a long cold winter in which the ice thickened to more than two feet, warm spring rains came, lots of them. For days on end it rained, turning the country to mush. The snow melted suddenly and poured into the river bed, lifting and shattering the ice and starting the whole surface moving at one time. Great bergs and floes reared up and dove under,

15

spinning and crowding each other up onto the shores and against the central pier of the bridge. They chewed away at the pier, tearing it apart, piece by piece, until there was no support left. The span sagged until it touched the moving ice, and then it broke in two. The halves swung downstream like the opening of a great gate, until coming to rest on the banks on either side. Most of the town had turned out to watch and everyone cheered the sheer brute force that had been exerted. Then the realization set in: there was no way across.

The summer that followed was exciting. We spent most of our spare time watching the new bridge being built and hanging around the construction camp, running errands, and being paid with chunks of raisin pie from the cook tent.

As we cross the new bridge, I look down at the brown sluggish stream. It's not as wide as it used to be, I'm sure. Swimming across it without stopping was an accomplishment to be proud of. Mm . . . yes, it must be narrower now.

Up the hill at the Shell station, we turn left onto a narrow gravel road and follow it for a mile to a junction. I think the instructions were to turn left again, so I do. The road gets narrower and winds down until we are back at the river and pass under the railroad bridge. It eventually ends at a farmyard. We backtrack to the junction and take the right-hand fork. Now I know where I am. We move along, and I untangle the threads of memory.

Amazingly enough, there are farm buildings that I recognize, still standing and looking much like they used to. Some are dwarfed by a new barn or a machine shed, but are still functional by the look of them. There are also farms where the buildings are gone, not a stick left standing: The Grahams' low gloomy shack; the Forbes' house that stood high on the hill, and Bill Gay's rambling log house where I was born. All are obliterated.

We turn left and cross the railroad tracks at a level crossing. To the left, about a quarter of a mile along the track, is where Robinson's Crossing once claimed distinction as being the last town on the line. There is not a trace of it now. In 1912, it was where the track ended and Father, a mule-skinner, became unemployed when construction work ceased. He wandered south three miles, found himself a homestead on the banks of the river and filed a claim to it. In 1914 he joined the army and went off to war. The little community was still there when he returned in 1918. The railroad had continued on in the meantime, eventually ending at Whitecourt, but the small cluster of buildings still housed a few families. My sister was born at Robinson's Crossing in 1919.

In the summer when I was ten years old, I was considered old enough to go to town by myself. I would walk the three miles to Robinson's and then follow the track to Sangudo, walking between the polished rails and listening to the singing of the telegraph wires alongside. On my return, with the mail and a few groceries in a gunny sack slung over my shoulder, I would ride on the train from Sangudo to Robinson's—if I had the five-cent fare—reducing my walk home by about two and a half miles. Occasionally, though, the conductor would forget I was on the train, and I would have to pull the emergency cord to bring it to a halt, sometimes a long way from the station.

What used to be bushland is now fields that stretch out in every direction, the marks of combines on them. It's hard to identify the individual farms, but by the distance we have come, I know that we must be at Olneys', although there is nothing left of their buildings to say so.

A strange pairing, the Olneys': he, a tall, cockney, ginger-mustached, steam-locomotive engineer from the British railway system; she, a Mother Hubbard type with iron-grey hair drawn back in a tight bun and dark upper-lip hair. She was a barmaid—and proud of it—from Blackpool. Unlikely qualifications, one might think, for farming an Alberta homestead, but they were successful, eventually cultivating more than a hundred acres of their quarter section. I remember their house, a one-room,

17

white-painted English cottage, surrounded by garden in which rhubarb, with stalks as thick as my arms and leaves like umbrellas, flourished in jungle-like profusion. And inside, from spring until freeze up, the pervasive yeasty aroma of fermenting rhubarb rose from earthen crocks and jugs sequestered behind the cookstove. Under the bed, in neat rows, were fruit jars full of the finished product. There were also jars full of a dark frothy brew Mrs. Olney called ale, made from grains from their own fields.

A story is told of a passer-by seeing the light from their window one cold winter evening, but getting no response to his rap at the door, opened it a crack and peered in. Fred Olney was sitting on the floor surrounded by empty fruit jars, singing "nearer my God to thee" and Mrs. Olney and Scotty Esplin, a bachelor neighbour, were dancing to it.

I cannot vouch for the authenticity of the story.

In those days, the 1920s, the road wound along the river bank passing through Olneys' yard. We seldom travelled it without stopping at Olneys' for a glass. Sometimes, if we were in a hurry, it was a stirrup cup handed up to the wagon seat. Sometimes with a caution:

"Try this, Jack. It's a new batch."

Father was not one to refuse a draught, even if it was only a day old.

Olney's liver gave out on him one day and his dying was long and painful in an Edmonton hospital. Mrs. Olney sold off the equipment at an auction—we bought some of the machinery—and moved to the next farm to keep house for Scotty Esplin. Within the year she perished, cremated in Scotty's small frame house that burned to the ground one night. Folks said that Fred Olney had reached down and reclaimed her.

On the other side of the road, along about a half a mile, is where Pudars lived. There is nothing left to identify where their buildings stood, either.

Pudar arrived there in about 1930. He walked, as the crow flies, straight through the bush from Mountain Park, arriving on our doorstep one afternoon, his clothes in tatters and his toes sticking out the fronts of his boots. He stayed for a meal, regaled us with his plans for the quarter section he had pre-empted sometime previously, and left wearing a pair of Father's cast-off boots. He built a low cottage out of small poles, plastered it with mud and before winter set in, moved his family into it. I can't remember how many children there were, but Leslie and George were roughly the same age as my brother and I.

That first winter must have been tough for them. They had a team of horses, a cow, a few chickens, and a single goose named Putty, but no garden or grain. Every few days, Leslie would show up at our place with a lard pail and a request to "borrow" enough grain to feed the chickens. It was a slim diet for the hens, but they survived, I guess—those that didn't get eaten.

Until Pudars came, we were pretty isolated. There were no close neighbors, except the Clarkes. The road ended at our place. We weren't even in a school district, so we didn't go to school. Leslie and George Pudar were the first kids we ever played with. They went to Poplar school, a one-roomer beyond Robinson's Crossing. They walked. It must have been about three miles each way. We were envious of them, but we couldn't go because we weren't in the school district.

The following summers, they would come to our place or we would go to theirs. Occasionally, Leslie and I would get sent to town for the mail and groceries aboard their old white mare, Lilly. She was a good natured plow horse with huge hooves, but she could lope along at a good pace when she felt like it. It wasn't easy to hang on to our grocery sacks and stay upright on her broad naked back, but it was more fun than walking.

The road forks, and I know we should take the one going straight ahead, but it looks narrow and wet—much like it did half a century ago. It doesn't look like a road over which to drive a modern automobile. We turn right, staying on the gravel.

19

"Where are you going?" asks my wife.

"I think I have to ask somebody. I'm sure that that is the road back there, but there may be a newer one. I'm afraid we will get stuck if we go down in there with anything less than a four-wheel drive or a tractor."

"There are some buildings up ahead," she says. "Maybe someone there knows something."

I turn off the road into a farmyard. Everything looks quiet—too quiet. I get the feeling that there is nobody home, although there is a pick-up truck in the yard. A dog uncurls itself from beside the porch and looks curiously at us. It doesn't bark; it just takes up a position halfway between the car and the porch. It doesn't look vicious, but I mistrust the appearance of any dog left by itself to look after the farm. I am hesitating, trying to decide whether to leave the safety of the car to go and knock on the door, when it opens and a tall man comes out and looks questioningly at us.

"Can I help you with something?" he asks, as I open the car door and get out. The dog says nothing.

"Yes, perhaps. I'm looking for the old Jones' homestead," I say. "Is that the road, the narrow one going down through the willows there?" I point in the general direction.

"The Jones' place . . . mm . . . " He looks puzzled. He is chewing on a toothpick. I guess I have disturbed his afternoon snack. "I don't remember anyone by that name living around here."

"They lived next to Clarkes, Nagy's place was next and Pudars were next to them on this side of the road," I say.

"Oh, yeah, well, Pudars' is right here, at the corner, and Clarkes' is right over there, but I don't remember anyone named Jones. How long ago did they live there?"

To get onto a first-person basis, I introduce myself.

"We left in 1932 and moved to town. We left the country in 1938 and went to the Coast."

I explain why we are here, that I just want to have a look at the old place. It's hard to make the whole idea sound sensible to a perfect stranger, but he seems to understand.

He speaks quietly, nods and smiles a little. He tells me his name is Bill Myndiuk and he has lived there all his life, but he doesn't remember us.

"Come on inside and talk to my mother. She may remember. She came here in 1937." He holds the door open for me. Mrs. Myndiuk, a slim attractive woman with grey hair, is sitting at the end of the kitchen table peeling apples and at the same time, keeping an eye on the television set in a corner of the living room. Her programme is on. I hope I'm not interrupting.

"Yes, I think I remember the name all right, but it was a long time ago and I was pretty young when I came here," she says.

We ask questions of one another and establish that we know a lot of the same people, but they are all people who remained in the country after we left. We also establish that she has a brother-in-law who lives only five blocks from us back home in Vernon, BC, and whom she has just been visiting a couple of weeks ago.

"Why don't you ask your wife, or whatever, to come on in," says Bill.

I go and fetch my wife from the car and introduce her. She and Mrs. Mynduik, by some obscure chemistry, immediately recognize each other as Ukrainians and some of the stiffness goes out of the conversation. We get down to good solid talk about what happened to whom, where does so-and-so live now and who married who. The kettle gets put on and tea is made. The next thing I know we are sitting at the kitchen table eating apple pie, drinking tea and talking like neighbours—which we were, I guess, away back when, although we didn't know it at the time.

"What are the chances of me driving the car down that narrow road to our old place?" I ask Bill.

"I wouldn't try it if I were you," he says. "It's pretty soft, but I'll run you down in the pickup. Mind you, I wouldn't offer if I was combining, but I've got a spare day so I'll take the time. It's only a few minutes."

I shouldn't have been surprised at the offer; that's the way people are out there on the Alberta farms. It has always been like that, but one tends to forget the open-heartedness of farming people. Urban living conditions one to think differently.

The pickup is a typical farm vehicle, a faded red under a layer of dust, bits of straw strewn on the floor and sticking out of the upholstery, and with a few bruises decorating the fenders. It is roomy, and my wife and I fit comfortably on the seat beside Bill.

I note a two-way radio hanging under the dash.

"Who do you talk to on the radio . . . neighbours, hired hands?" I ask.

"It doesn't work," he says. "A few years ago, everybody got them . . . thought it was a good idea. Just another fad, though. They broke down and nobody wanted to spend the time or the money to get them fixed. I doubt any of them work now, but it was kind of nice at the time."

We bump down through the willows on the old road.

"The old Clarke place is just over the hill there," Bill says. He wheels the truck into the stubble field and grinds carefully across it to the brow of the hill. I look down on an old log building with its back broken and things growing up through it. Memory comes flooding back. That derelict pile of logs becomes a barn with a team of horses in it, a black and a grey, Bill and Bess. The house was over there, to the left. The fences and outbuildings arrange themselves into Clarkes' farmyard.

Jim Clarke, so the story went, walked, hoboing his way north from Alabama, arriving sometime during the first great war. He filed on the land and shortly afterwards, Mrs. Clark came, by what route or from where I don't know. It was never discussed. They had two daughters. The eldest was the same age as my sister and the youngest the same age as me.

Although we lived side by side, we were never friends. Jim Clarke and Father didn't get along. I never did know all of the reasons why.

"I've never known anyone by the name of Clarke who amounted to anything," Father was wont to say.

Mother was a little more lenient and occasionally she would take us, and we would visit for an afternoon. The eldest daughter contracted tuberculosis and lay in bed in a tent in the dooryard all one summer. Everybody expected her to die by autumn, but she fooled them; she got better. She grew up, went to school, and I heard—I don't remember where—that she eventually got married.

"There's supposed to be a grave there somewhere," Bill says.

"Yes, it's over on the river bank," I say. I know exactly where it is. I'm sure I could walk right to it. It is the grave of a third child who survived only a few days, a week at most. A life so brief that it never found its way into any official record. The last time I saw the small mound, there was a little cross and a few flowers decorating it. Now, I doubt there is anything remaining above or below ground.

We move on, bumping across the field, back to the road.

It has changed a little. It used to bear left down through a ravine, cross the creek on a log bridge, and then climb a hill to our farmyard. Now it just goes straight ahead, crosses the creek over a culvert and ends just about where our house stood. Bill is a little dubious about driving the pickup through some soft spots near the creek, so we get out and walk the last hundred yards.

I stand where I haven't stood for sixty-two years. Under my feet is the heavy clay that, until my father arrived, had lain undisturbed since the last glacier plowed its way across it, peopled only by the Cree, who followed the river and dwelt seasonally on the benchland south of where our buildings stood. Some of their lodge poles, slim poplars silvered with age, were still standing there when I became old enough to be aware of such things. And once when I was very young, there were painted ponies, their heads over our fence, passing the time of day with our old work horses.

Even though it has had several owners since we abandoned it, I still feel a sense of possessing this land. There is an attachment to the earth that I can't explain. An urge comes to reach down and take some of it in my hands and feel it, but I don't; I'm afraid it will smack too much of Hollywood. Alone, I might have.

So what now? I see the questioning looks on the faces of my wife and Bill. There is nothing here, nothing that they can see, at least. The buildings are gone; not the slightest depression or hump indicates that they once stood here. The marks of tractors and machines are unswerving as they cross the spot where I was conceived. I really don't want to do anything special. I would just like to sit for awhile, look at the contours of the land and the way the sky meets it and remember, to soak up the feeling of a long time ago. I can't do that, of course, not while two people stand impatiently watching me.

We ramble across the field and look down at the river. The water is brown and runs slow, as it always did. Just below where we are standing is where I learned to swim and where I caught my first fish, a muscular pike that nearly tore the willow pole from my hands. Wolf willow and chokecherry still grow in profusion on the steep banks.

Bill points back across the creek to the sloping field that was once Clarkes'. A big coyote, its nose to the ground, is drifting across the stubble, searching for mice. A tingle goes up my spine and the hair on the back of my neck prickles. The coyotes are still here, then. It is good to know that. I remember being thrilled, but at the same time, scared stiff as I lay in bed with the covers pulled tight under my chin, listening to them sing close around our house. I think, good on you, coyote, you and I have something in common; your ancestors and I both dwelt here when this was mostly wilderness.

Bill has managed to get the pickup across the creek. We get in and he shifts into bull low and the pickup crawls up the hill where I first felt skis glide under my feet and where I first fell and made a sitz mark. We come to a north/south road where

where none used to be, and we turn left towards the hogback. The hogback is a gunsight-shaped piece of land formed by the river winding back on itself and leaving a thin, knife-edged ridge connecting a brushy knob to the benchland. It was like that when we lived here, but the river has worn through the ridge and the knob has become an island. It's still called the "hogback," although it isn't one anymore. We can't drive right to it, but we stand on the bench above looking down on it.

"There used to be an old coal mine down there," I say.

"It's still there," Bill says. "Do you want to go down and have a look at it?" I would like to. I am curious, and I'm sure Bill would have found a way to get us there, but I decide it is not worth the effort.

The mine was operated for two or three winters in the late twenties by Fred Teer and a man named Brown whose first name I have forgotten, but whose daughters, Edna and Maggie, went to school in Sangudo when I did. Both men farmed the stony benchland across the river from town, ground so poor that only a bare existence could be wrung from it. They turned to the river and sought a few extra winter dollars by mining coal from its banks. They didn't have title to the land they mined; they just squatted there and dug.

For weeks at a time during the short cold days of January and February, they burrowed into the bank, picking out the low-grade coal from a pit that sometimes collapsed on them for want of shoring. At night, they huddled in a shack thrown together out of sawmill slabs. Their horses sheltered in a grove of spruce trees. A sleigh box that ran close to a ton, freighted down the surface of the river, would fetch two dollars in town.

It was a dangerous trek down-river. Depending on the weather and the temperature of subterranean springs rising from the river bed, the strength of the ice could vary from day to day, and there was no telling where the weak spots were. It was not unusual during a winter for someone to lose a team through the ice. It was a trip fraught with peril.

We would hear the jingle of trace chains and the squeak of loaded sleigh runners and run to the river bank to watch them pass, two bearded figures, black as the load they were freighting, hunched on the front of their sleigh box behind frost-encrusted horses. We would holler and wave, and sometimes a weary hand would be raised in reply.

They both left the country a few years after we did. I don't know what happened to Brown, but I heard that Teer was murdered in Toronto.

The afternoon is wearing on and apart from the fields that roll on south and west, there is nothing much more I can say that I really want to look at. There are things, though, things I haven't told anyone about, and I won't. I may come back here sometime.

We head back for Mynduik's buildings. We talk about farming in this part of Alberta, the way it was and the way it is now. Bill has to take courses in heavy machinery mechanics, just to keep his equipment rolling. He has a machine inventory in the hundreds of thousands of dollars. He knows nothing of horses: he doesn't own one, never has.

A young coyote peers out from behind hay bales lying in the field. He is all ears and curious. Just looking at him makes me feel good inside. Some things remain unchanged.

It's hard to thank Bill. He's gone out of his way to help satisfy a crazy yearning in a perfect stranger. We shake, and we take our leave down the gravel road.

At the corner, I look over to where Nagys lived, just over there on the river bank. They were between Clarkes and Olneys.

Dczso Nagy came from Hungary in the late twenties and bought the odd-shaped tract of land on which stood a small weathered cottage and nothing else. A thick-set, tired-looking man, he walked with a limp, his foot splaying sideways from having caught a piece of shrapnel during the war, a gift from our side of that conflict. His family followed a year or so later.

The youngest daughter Zeta a toddler, died on the ship during the crossing of the Atlantic and was buried at sea without Dezso knowing about it until they debarked from the train at Robinson's. Within the year, however, a new Zeta was born. There were two older daughters, Barbara and Helen—both big strapping girls.

Nagy and his brother-in-law, Andy, worked for us briefly, clearing a strip of land along the river.

There is a motel on the edge of town, down on the flats where we hunted rabbits. We take a room for the night. The owner is a newcomer and knows little about the community or its history. We ask about a place to eat, and she recommends a restaurant on the main street. I had noticed it when we entered town.

Beside it is a false-fronted building that belonged to my father. It was his office and what passed for the local court house. Outwardly, it hasn't changed. It has been moved, though, from the side street where it crouched behind the hardware store. In it Father, a Justice of the Peace, held court and tried people for assorted misdemeanors. His biggest case, one that split the town right down the middle, resulted in the conviction and the sentencing of a farmer to jail—thirty days, for lighting a fire that burned up half the country. Father made a few lasting enemies out of that one.

The restaurant is remodelled, tastefully decorated and the staff is friendly. We get into a long conversation with the young woman who tends the bar. It is early and business is slow, so she has time to kill. I find out a lot of things about the town and how it has evolved from where it was when we left.

It is not a bad meal.

There used to be two places to eat, Mrs. Sherrington's and Jim Mah's cafe. Mrs. Sherrington was there first. Her husband Charlie, a short fat bombastic man, ran the first garage in town. It had two pumps with glass reservoirs on top out front. There was something about those pumps . . .

It seemed we couldn't pass them without grabbing the big handles and pumping the glasses full. Charlie auctioneered and had a trucking business on the side. I worked for him hauling hay and grain when I first quit school. He owned the first Ford-V8 truck in town. I worked for Mrs. Sherrington while I was still going to school, splitting wood and filling the vast wood box in her kitchen, a job that took most of my after-school time. She paid me twenty-five cents a week and usually admonished me to put something aside for a rainy day as she doled out my pay from her apron pocket.

Jim Mah, a slim Chinese with a wide smile and an uncommon gift of butchering the English language, built a cafe on the corner across from Sherringtons'. He did so despite opposition from a few of the more red-neck burghers who saw him as a threat to something or other.

"Damn Chinamen, all they eat is a bit of rice. No white man can compete with them," was a typical grumbled comment when Jim first showed up. The thing was, Mah had hard cash, money enough to put up a building, so there was a scramble for carpentry jobs, even though he was Chinese. Nobody was that red-necked.

He persevered, and it wasn't long before the rough interior— decorated with mirrors and calendars depicting colourful Chinese scenes and exotic birds—with a few booths on one side and a full-length counter along the other was the place to go for coffee after a meeting or a hockey or baseball game. It was where we hung out and spent our nickels and dimes on bottles of pop and pie. He had a menu a yard long, and by some sleight-of-hand, could call up just about anything on it. Over time he became part of the village mosaic, and even those whose opposition was the most vociferous in the beginning could be found sipping coffee in a booth at Jim Mah's.

It is quiet in the motel, as quiet as it used to be at night when I lay in bed, only about a block away in our rough frame cottage. The odd truck rumbles past over on the highway.

The sound, muted by the distance, is markedly different from the clopping of hooves and the rattling of buggy wheels that used to come singing past our door in the velvet darkness of late summer evenings after the beer parlour closed.

There is a laundromat near the motel, and since we have been on the road for a week the laundry bag is full. The following morning seems an opportune time to attend to it.

"Why don't you go and wander around town by yourself while I do the laundry," my wife suggests.

I make the usual gestures, but seize the opportunity.

I wander up the street towards the old school.

The Anglican church never was a pretentious building. A small frame structure without steeple, column or pediment, it nestled among struggling trees adjacent to the Legion hall. The minister Angus Devere Hunt was a tall, cadaverous, scholarly Englishman. He prowled his huge diocese in a mud-spattered Hudson Terraplane and conducted services on Sunday afternoons. The organ, an ancient foot-treadled instrument, was coaxed into life each week by Mother, who had to pump mightily to extract sufficient volume to lead the congregation. It was much too feeble to compete with the rich baritone of the Reverend Hunt, whose voice could be heard almost to the river, soaring above the combined output of organ and the choir.

The building is showing its age. It is still the same blue-grey colour, but it needs painting and the grass needs cutting. I wonder who the minister is now.

The Legion hall is no longer that. I notice a sign on what used to be the Masonic hall that proclaims the Legion now occupies it. The old Legion hall has become a dwelling. There are curtains at the window and flowers out front. It looks a little dilapidated.

It was built in 1936 when Father was one of the movers and shakers in the Legion. It was a pretty rough edifice but it had one of the grandest grand openings ever seen in that part of the country. Lieutenant Governor Walsh and a contingent of frontiersmen made the tortuous journey from Edmonton by touring car over mud roads to cut the ribbon and conduct the dedication ceremony. A great beginning, but one that seems to have ended rather ignominiously. I wonder why.

The last time I saw this building was a few nights before we caught the train for Vancouver in 1938. Our schoolmates threw a party for us in it.

Across the street is a seniors' drop-in centre. There must be some old-timers in there, I think. I walk over and try the door, but it is locked.

"Good morning," I say to an elderly woman with a shopping bag, who is moving tentatively along the broken sidewalk and who nods at me. "Have you lived here very long?"

"All my life," she replies proudly without a hint of suspicion as to why a complete stranger would be asking.

"I'm looking for people who remember the town back in the thirties," I say. "I lived here then."

"Is that right." she says. "Well, I was a . . ." She tells me her family name. The wheels spin backwards . . . I know who this woman is, and I know things about her that are best not remembered. I tell her who I am, but she looks blank. Perhaps she does remember me, though.

"Well, I must be getting on. I have a number of things to do," she says and continues her careful way down the street.

The United church is new. The old one, built by the Reverend Douglas McTavish who like Jesus was a carpenter before he was a minister, has been demolished and replaced by one of a more modern design. The manse has been refurbished and looks cared for. The Uniteds are doing better than the Anglicans by the look of it. It was always so, except that McTavish had to service his diocese in a model T Ford tourer, a lesser automobile than a Hudson Terraplane.

Back on the main street I look for the barber shop. Just for old-time's sake, I think I might get my hair cut. The building where it used to be is now a beauty salon, and it is closed until noon according to a sign in the window.

When Herschel Korber ran the barber shop, it was also a pool hall and was open all day every day except Sunday. It needed to be; it took forever to get a haircut. Herschel wasn't the swiftest barber in the land and since he only cut between his turns at the pool table, the best part of an afternoon could be used up sitting on the padded board suspended across the arms of the barber chair.

There were the regulars: Charlie Sherrington, Gus Anderson, Pat Kerr and a few more. In summer when the doors stood open, the click of pool balls was audible out on the board walk and Charlie's plaintive "Gaaaaad dammit" when he missed a shot, could be heard the full length of main street. I don't see any sign that says 'pool hall.'

I walk on down the street and around the corner, past where Keely's store used to be and his house next to it. Both buildings look abandoned. Ferrol Keely and I were friends. I was eight days older than her and we always made a thing of it. I may still be eight days older than her, come to think of it. I wonder what happened to her.

Just about where the village office is, Ernie Dumbril's drug store stood. He sold patent medicines, phonograph needles, violin strings, and for a long time he was the only purveyor of ice cream in town—the main reason for us kids to go there. He wasn't the friendliest person. Something in his past had soured him. He usually came out of his rooms in the back, looking rumpled and mouthing imprecations at being disturbed. He had no fingers and had difficulty managing the ice cream scoop. There were various stories circulating about how he lost his fingers. The one that was given most credence was that he had at one time been a heavy drinker, and once when he had consumed more than was prudent, had spent a cold winter night passed out in a snow bank. His fingers froze and had to be amputated.

There are few people moving on the streets as I wander back to the laundromat where my wife has just finished drying the clothes.

"Well, have you seen enough?" she asks.

"I think so," I say. "Without staying for a week or more and really digging up people, there's not a whole lot more I want to see."

"Is there nobody you want to find and talk to?"

"There is one, Lloyd Conrad. He and I used to get on pretty well. I used to deliver his papers for him. I know where he lives; the woman in the office told me. It's on the way out of town. We could stop in and see if he's home."

Lloyd's place is just off the highway after it crossed the tracks heading back on 757. It's where the fairgrounds were almost seventy years ago.

It is a nice looking place, a neat and tidy place. Lloyd would have that kind of a place; he was that kind of a person even when he was a kid. There is a camper van and a tractor in the yard, but it is quiet. The only thing moving is a squirrel scurrying around on the porch. Nobody answers my knock. I write a note and stick it in the door, just to let him know I remember him. I turn to get back in the car and glance across the tracks to the town.

There is something permanent there. It will always be there, I think, and there is comfort in that. I can go on my way knowing it will still be there if I ever decide to come back.

We head back toward Highway 16 between the muskegs and the yellow fields. The soft, rounded country slides past. It is friendly country, peopled with friendly folk. I have not uncovered any earth-shaking truths that will make my life different from here on, but I have found that everything is pretty much as I remember it, and for that I am thankful. I'm glad I came.

2 • The Arrival

THE PEMBINA RIVER RISES AT CADOMIN, IN THE FOOTHILLS ON THE Alberta side of the Rocky Mountains. It starts as a trickle of meltwater from the same patch of snow that spawns the McLeod and the Brazeau rivers. It tumbles freely from the high ground and then slows and snakes its way in leisurely fashion, northeast through the parkland of west central Alberta to its confluence with the Athabaska. In its wanderings it passed our homestead, flowing generally along its eastern border.

Seen from its banks—a couple of hundred yards distant—in the 1920s, it would have been easy to imagine that our farm buildings had arrived there by struggling upward through the soil, like mushrooms after a rainy night, their organic upthrusting appearing as vertical extensions of the land. They were, if the truth were known, going the other way, sinking slowly into it.

As typical farm buildings they were on the low side of average, which wasn't very good—amateurish, even shoddy, some might say. They were all simple rectangular structures without adornment, their materials taken from close at hand. The house and barn were of crudely-hewn poplar logs without dovetailing at the corners or other skilled joinery, the logs just notched and saddled—the simplest form of tying walls together. The house roof and gables were shingled, but those on the barn had nothing more than overlapping rough-sawn boards to keep out the weather. About the only manufactured items used anywhere were a few nails and window glass. There was plaster between the logs, made from lime and sand, an admixture that readily fell out when baked in the summer sun or cracked in the winter cold when the logs flexed. On the barn, as a temporary measure to keep out winter draughts, it was often replaced with fresh cow manure that froze solid and lasted until spring.

Little or no effort had gone into the appearance of the pig and chicken houses. They were low gloomy huts made of round logs with the bark still on and with sawmill slabs for roofs, the first layer laid flat-side up and the second laid face down over the cracks. The animals and birds that occupied these uninsulated shelters depended on their own pelage and plumage and on heaps of straw to keep the chill from their bodies in winter temperatures that regularly plummeted far below freezing.

Where the buildings were exposed to the sun, all had weathered to a silver grey, but on the north sides and in the shade under the eaves, they had browned to a weak coffee colour. Nowhere had a paintbrush ever touched them.

Westward beyond them the land climbed, a gentle rounding of an ancient escarpment, not high, but high enough to be called a hill and the only one anywhere around. Aeons ago it was the bank of the river that, over time, had shrunk to a tenth of its width and reseated itself in a narrower channel. Southward was the flat bench that had been riverbed, its clayey loam deposited there by the glaciers as they departed. It extended all the way to the hogback and further, forested with poplar, birch and willow, lush growth standing tight as broom straws except where it had given way to Father's axe. On the north side, down below the buildings, was the creek flowing through a brushy gully that it had scoured for itself and that widened as it neared the river. The barn perched on its lip and sagged toward it.

The house had been started in 1912, its sill-logs laid

without benefit of cement or stone to separate them from the ground. It was the first house Father had ever built. At the time, he saw no need to construct anything more resplendent than was absolutely necessary to qualify as a dwelling—as defined in the land pre-emption act. It was not tall-tree country and logs of any length were not plentiful. Those that had any length were mature enough also to have considerable girth, and since he had to haul them to the site and hoist them in place by himself, he had good reason keep the dimensions modest. He measured with his axe handle. When he later measured with a rule, it came in at sixteen by fourteen feet—outside dimensions. When he had got it high enough to walk around in with his hat on—he was only five-foot, six inches on a good day, so it wasn't very high—he put a sloping shed roof on it and topped it with sod. He furnished it with a stove and a bunk.

He lived in it spasmodically, but it was a long way from anywhere and too quiet for him to remain there for very long at one time. Since he owned neither horse nor cow, cat nor dog, there was nothing to keep him there except the pre-emption requirements.

Gregarious by nature and accustomed to the companionship of railroad construction workers, he quickly became lonely, and frequently went looking for like souls in such places as Edmonton, Calgary and Winnipeg, returning just often enough to satisfy the land office inspectors that he actually was living on the place. While in residence, he began carving fields out of the dense growth. His only implements were an axe and a saw. Needless to say, it was slow going and fuelled with only lukewarm enthusiasm. He had no great ambition to put down roots in this isolated bend of the river. He was first and foremost a railroader, and homesteading was something to while away the days until construction work recommenced.

Father, christened John Evan Lewis Jones, called Jack and seldom, if ever, addressed as John, was a barrel-chested

Welshman with the black hair and ruddy complexion typical of that race. He was virtually uneducated. He had gone through the third-form twice by age thirteen—the highest level of learning available in the village school—equipping him to read, write and do basic arithmetic, but leaving him knowing little beyond that.

Conditioned by the black fears and beliefs of a family rooted deeply in ancient Britain, he paid homage to many and varied signs and symbols, and often practicality and good sense were overridden by some whim of superstition. He would never start anything on a Friday; if a black cat crossed his path he would go the other way to the point that he wouldn't have a black cat on the place; he would not tolerate putting new shoes on the table, nor would he abide anyone paring their fingernails on Sunday; calamity would befall if a dark-haired girl was to whistle in the house. All of these and many more, he held as bad luck. He worshipped the number thirteen and any multiple thereof.

His arrival at the homestead was the culmination of a tortuous journey that had begun in Llanvethrine, Wales in 1903. At age seventeen he had left home for Canada, much to the dismay of his family whose members—none of whom had ever ventured further than the corner pub—could not conceive of a journey so vast. Although having lived for generations no more than thirty miles from the ocean, none of them had ever seen it. It is also possible that lurking in the backs of their minds was a latent belief that the world really was flat—that is if they thought about it at all—and were fearful that their Jack would fall off the end of it. He didn't tell them where he was going, for the simple reason he didn't know—other than to Canada. He caught a train for Liverpool, a boat to Montreal, and another train to Winnipeg where he stalled for want of money to proceed further; he had only a single dollar left in his pocket. Why he had pushed on as far as Winnipeg he couldn't explain except that it was in the middle of the country and seemed a good place to strike out from in any direction.

The skills he had to offer were those of the Welsh farms, handed down through a family that had worked as farmers and gardeners for generations, always on the estates of others, never owning anything. He had grown up knowing how to drive and care for horses. In a small country where every blade of grass and every kernel of grain was husbanded, a chore delegated to small boys was the doling out of fodder, a measure at a time as it was eaten, to the draught horses, the gentle giants that were the prime movers of the Welsh countryside. Grooming and driving them was a natural extension of this chore. Teamsters were in demand in Winnipeg, so he landed a job almost immediately, driving a freight wagon within the city.

He made friends easily, and as was natural, they came from those engaged in the management of horses and the vehicles they drew. The city seethed with every conceivable conveyance, from light buggies drawn by lively carriage horses to heavy freight wagons pulled by draught animals weighing more than a ton. Nothing moved except by horse power.

A driver named John Richardson became his close friend and mentor. John was an expatriate Englishman and newly married. Mary, his wife, was a pretty fun-loving woman whom he had met before leaving England and married in Winnipeg without gaining parental approval. In the words of her sister, Ann: "My poor sister, Mary. She ran away to Canada to marry that dreadful John Richardson." Ann, however, did have to admit that Richardson was a handsome devil and that her sister was not entirely unhappy with the choice she had made. They had a house in Elmwood, a suburb of Winnipeg, and they welcomed young Jack into it. For a while, he boarded with them and then, off and on for the next few years, stayed with them whenever he was in Winnipeg.

Jack was just one of many young men seeking their fortunes in Winnipeg—at that time a bustling frontier town—and theirs was a boisterous, hard-drinking fraternity whose members cared little for permanence, instead seeking adventure. The railroad, upon which much of the city's economy depended, offered that. Jack became a railroader, again driving horses and mules sometimes as many as twenty-six at a time (one of the magic multiples of thirteen to which he paid obeisance) hauling earth moving machinery and freight wagons. He worked west into the Rocky Mountains on what was then called the Brazeau line, and south into the Crowsnest Pass where he was put in charge of the stables—a position that gave him the grandiose title of 'Barn Boss'—caring for hundreds of draught animals. And always, when a break came, it was back to Winnipeg where he stayed with the Richardsons.

A single event in 1908, would alter forever, the devil-may-care course that he was set upon, and influence the lives of the players in the pageant of his life that followed a few years later.

John Richardson was killed. The circumstances leading to his death were cloaked in mumbled half-truths and never convincingly explained. The story that became record and was given most credence by those in the know was that he was driving a freight wagon when the horses bolted and he was thrown to the ground and run over by its wheel. The talk bruited about among the teamsters was that the wagon was one of several owned by a brewery, and that Richardson had sampled too freely of the company's wares to the point that he was unable to stay upright on it. He was dead nonetheless, and it was left to Jack, who hurried back to Winnipeg, to help Mary pack up her belongings and, by then, two children—a girl and a boy born in 1907 and 1908—and return to England.

Four years later in 1912, Jack was west of Edmonton building roadbed on a branch line that would eventually reach into British Columbia. Two miles west of Sangudo, roadbed construction stalled. A massive wooden bridge had to be built to span the Pembina Valley, which at that point was nearly a mile wide. It was a task that would take more than' two years to complete. Until trains could get across to bring steel rails, ties, and work crews, track laying was held up. Rather than let grading get too far ahead, it was halted and the work force laid off. A collection of log buildings sprang up to house those waiting for construction to resume. Some with families settled in with the intent of letting the railroad move on without them. The village became known as Robinson's Crossing and, for a while, it boasted a hotel, a store, a doctor and a bootlegger. Who Robinson was is lost in time.

Left without a paying job, Jack wandered southward three miles and located a quarter section of fertile land in a bend of the river to be had for a five-dollar pre-emption fee and a promise to carry out specified assessment work: build a house, establish a year-round water supply, and clear an acre of land a year for a period of five years, at which time he could, with a further fee of twenty-five dollars, obtain clear title.

Had he been left to his own devices he may have followed through with all of these requirements, but it is doubtful. He had begun the same venture a few years earlier, south of Calgary in the heart of what was to become one of the richest oil fields in Canada. He abandoned the project in favour of the life of a railroader without ever gaining title to the land or, more important, what lay below it. However, events in Europe made it possible for him to acquire title to this latest homestead without doing the assessment work.

War broke out in 1914 and Jack, along with hundreds of others with lingering loyalties to Great Britain, hastened off to join the army without so much as a backward glance at his labour of the last two years. Because he had enlisted, the land department waved their requirements and guaranteed his title assuming, of course, that he didn't get killed and was able to return and take possession.

He joined the Fifty-First Canadian Infantry Battalion in Edmonton and was shipped overseas shortly after, one in a troopship full of enthusiastic, singing, young men off to teach the Kaiser a lesson. In a matter of weeks, they were in Aldershot, southwest of London, where the battalion settled in to train for war in France and Belgium. No amount of training, however, would prepare them for the horror of the trenches and the hand-to-hand combat they immediately encountered in Flanders; certainly not war games in the peaceful English countryside and parade-ground marching with rifles at the slope.

On leaves during those first few months, Jack entrained north to Morpeth, Northumberland where Mary Richardson was teaching school. Although Mary was four years older, their relationship developed into more than that of just friends, and later while Jack was on a leave from France, they were married in the chapel at Llanvethrine, Wales. It was July 1916.

Jack returned to France and the trenches. He didn't talk much about this part of the war, but it is known from things inadvertently let drop by those who knew him—two who survived, Billy Renny and Jimmy Ostler, who shared the same dug-outs and shell holes with him—that he was a sniper and as such would have seen, over the dulled sights of his Lee-Enfield rifle, the shattering impact of bullets taking the lives of human beings—bullets that he had directed. The fact that they were Germans and the enemy did little to mitigate the act of killing, and memories of such would torment him for the rest of his days. That he could be an efficient sniper indicates that there was an underlying ruthlessness about him. He was actually an odd mixture: an amalgam of insecurity, fear, bravery, superstition, hail-fellow and truculence. He was a hard taskmaster, as anyone who ever worked for him could attest, and a martinet to those around him.

In the winter of 1917, he was wounded. Fragments from a bursting shell lacerated his thigh. There was no structural damage, but it was a severe wound and it became infected beyond the capabilities of the front line hospitals to cope. He was shipped back to England to a hospital at Purfleet, Essex. He never did return to France.

Mary and the two children moved to Essex to be near where he was convalescing. A short time later, Mary became ill with tuberculosis. She died in August 1918.

Jack was now mired in a situation from which there was no easy way to extricate himself: he was only thirty two, uneducated, had never had to worry about anyone but himself, had been wounded, gassed, and shell shocked—a term used at that time to describe the trauma resulting from exposure to prolonged artillery fire. He was the sole guardian of two orphaned children (ages ten and eleven) whom he had not fathered, but whom he had to provide for; he was being shipped by the army back from whence he came and, once there, he had nowhere to go but his sod-roofed shack in Alberta. It was time for sober thought.

Mary's sister, Ann (also a school teacher) with a strong sense of duty toward her sister's children had in the meantime been looking after them in her lodgings in South Shields and had actually enrolled them in school for a few months. Jack, a handsome young adventurer from the colonies, beguiled her with tales of his ranch in Alberta—by his own admission, he gilded the lily, laying it on pretty thick. One such piece of nonsense that surfaced years later during a time of recrimination:

"Come with me," he'd said, "to sunny Alberta, where the sun shines on both sides of the fence and apples and oranges grow in clusters and it's summer all the time."

If she was actually taken in by this fiction, she never admitted it. All she would say was, "He was pretty persuasive." And usually with a little smile. However, the upshot was that she agreed to marry him and accompany him and the children to Canada. They were married (a civil ceremony) in London in October 1918, two months after Mary's death. The ring, a plain gold band, purchased at Bensons of London, would be the only ring of any kind that Ann would ever wear. Two weeks later just before the Armistice was signed, they left Liverpool for Montreal.

They would never return, and neither would ever again see any of their families.

It was an illogical union. The only common thread that bound them was two children who belonged to neither of them. They were not in love. In fact, they didn't know each other very well. It was a marriage of convenience: Jack, who needed a mother for the children he had acquired by default, and Ann, who was resolved not to let them disappear into the Canadian wilderness without one. Ann had examined her options and found them to be few and unexciting: stay in post-war England as an old-maid schoolteacher or find somebody to marry—for which, until now, substantial offers were singularly lacking. She opted for adventure with Jack. She was twenty-nine, five feet one inch tall and weighed in at just over one hundred pounds.

It would be hard to conceive of a more unlikely foursome to send off into the Alberta outback than these. They had been brought together by chance and now were compelled to stay together by sheer necessity. The only one who had any qualifications whatsoever for a life in the bush was Jack, and he had been debilitated by four years of war. Ann didn't have the vaguest idea of what she was going to. She had nothing more to go on than the glowing verbal portraits of the golden west that Jack had painted. She had never lived outside the city, had always been looked after, at home or in lodgings and had never had to cook, clean or do laundry—other than perhaps her own underwear. As she said, "I didn't even know how to boil water for tea." The children didn't know what to expect; they had always lived in cities. Nancy (the eldest) and John, although having been born in Winnipeg, had only vague memories of it. They had recently lost their mother; they had acquired a father they hardly knew and were somewhat hostile to—he hadn't been around all that much, being either in army quarters, in the trenches of France or in hospital. They had become accustomed to living in England and had no desire to return to

Canada, much less with two people they didn't know very well.

The trip from Liverpool to Montreal took ten days on a ship crowded with weary servicemen who had weathered the war in France, Belgium, and wherever else, many with newly acquired British and French wives and more recently yet, the children of these unions, and all of their accoutrements. There were also those maimed for life and destined for Canadian hospitals.

After that, there was the wearisome trip in a troop train across most of a continent. They finally arrived in Calgary where Jack went through the demobilization process. He was freed from the army on Nov. 22, 1918. He had never risen beyond the rank of private.

They immediately entrained north to Edmonton and then west to Robinson's Crossing. By this time the bridge across the Pembina, a lattice of timber reaching out from both sides and joined by web of steel across the river itself, had been completed and the tracks had moved on. The end of steel was now at Whitecourt, Alberta. Robinson's Crossing was largely abandoned and the residents, being people of the railroad, had followed its westerly progression.

It was a cold late-November day—the snow had held off, but the ground was frozen—when their baggage was unloaded at the station: a converted boxcar without heat. There were few people about and no one Jack knew. While Ann and the children waited, huddled in their inadequate English clothing next to their trunks, Jack scouted around until he found a team of horses and a wagon he could borrow. They loaded their possessions and set out over a scarcely discernible wheel track to the homestead Jack had last seen four years ago.

It is difficult to imagine a more inhospitable end to their multi-thousand mile trek. To Jack, it was not a joyous homecoming, and to the rest, it was a shock. The shack that had been built in 1912 had suffered the ravages of time and

neglect: the sod roof had partially collapsed; the windows
were broken; the chinking had fallen out from between the
logs; the door was open, and the room was full of blown
debris. Young poplars had re-established themselves, forming
an almost impenetrable barrier in front of the door. There was
no possibility of inhabiting it.

They were cold, hungry, disheartened and nearing exhaus-
tion. Ann was pregnant and not feeling well and the November
daylight was rapidly fading. Something had to be done, and
soon, but what? Should they go back to Robinson's? It would
be pitch dark long before they got there . . . there were no
hotels . . . they didn't know anyone . . .

Across the river about half a mile away, a light appeared
in the window of a log house scarcely discernible in the gloom
of the late afternoon. It was invitingly near and made the
decision for them. Jack turned the horses toward it. He knew
the banks were steep and brushy and he wasn't sure if the
stream had ever been forded anywhere close at hand, but
being late November, he figured the water was as low as it
would get. Without daring to think too much about it, he took
a chance. Using all of his skill as a teamster, he worked the
team and wagon southward through the trees and under-
brush to where the land fell away and the banks could be
negotiated with less of a threat. He headed the horses down
to the broad stream that already had fringes of ice forming
along its edges and coerced them into it. They all hung on as
the wheels bumped over the stony bed and then up the other
side. It was a hard pull in the stony ground, and the horses
scrambled mightily to draw the heavily laden wagon to the
benchland above. They made it safely, but for years, they
would wonder at the foolhardiness of such a crossing and
thank whichever saint was on duty that afternoon for letting
them get away with it. It was November 26—the second multiple of thirteen. Guided by the light spilling from the window
and the barking of a dog, they found the house and pulled up
in the dooryard. It was occupied by Earl and Irma Lowery, a

young recently-married couple who were aghast at the appearance of the wagon and its occupants from the direction of the river.

Lowerys took them in, an unbelievable gesture of open-heartedness. Their cottage, although spacious for the time, was not designed to accommodate four extra people and their baggage at a moment's notice.

They stayed the winter.

3 • The Settlers

THERE WOULD BE MORE SEVERE WINTERS, AND LONGER ONES, BUT none that the four people crammed like herrings in a box with Lowerys in their log house would remember more vividly than that of 1918–19. They would remember, but they wouldn't talk about it—not until years afterward when they had given up and moved away. Even then, there were hurts that were still tender and would never be healed completely.

Theirs had been a hurried departure, almost a furtive scurrying about to become a family so that the Canadian army would transport them to Canada. They had uprooted themselves—all in a few weeks—from the brick and stone permanence of a sizeable seaport teeming with people and the creature comforts they had always taken for granted to be transplanted into this land. To all appearances it was barren of life and warmth. Grimed though it was with smoke and coal dust, South Shields was home and suddenly they yearned for it, dreariness and all. Here, it mattered not which direction they looked, there was only snow and the grey of winter trees. Family and all of the cultural niceties that had sculpted their lives had been traded for isolation and loneliness. There were no church steeples piercing the skyline, no schools, no theatres, no shops. In fact, there were no buildings of any kind, other than the rough log cottage they shared with Lowerys, the stable, and a few low outbuildings. There were no people: no relatives, no friends, no strangers. The only living things for miles around were those of the farm and the animals of the forest, animals that they fully believed were lurking in wait to eat them if they stepped outside the door.

It took a while to sink in that this was not just a temporary stopover that in a while they would not continue on to the safety and comfort of some urban centre. This was it . . . the end of the road. There was no going on or going back. And then came despondency, despair, and fear. They cast about for escape, whetting their anger on Jack, the man who had brought them here, the man who was to become my father. "Why could they not go home to England? Would it not be better to live in Edmonton or Calgary? . . . anywhere, but not here." There would be no escape; they realized it after awhile, no matter how much they railed at Father. He too was trapped; he didn't have the wherewithal to leave, and anyway, there was nowhere else to go. Returning to England was impossible as was living in Edmonton or Calgary. All he knew was railroad construction work and that was no longer an option. There was nothing for it but to dig in, shrug off their fears and begin learning to survive. And they would survive and discover in themselves the ability to cope, but none would ever be happy and fulfilled—not throughout their lives.

The snow had come out of a leaden sky the day after they arrived. At first, soft pretty flakes like drifting goose-down and then hard scouring pellets driven slantwise out of the northwest and along the river valley, riding a gale that rattled the house as it sucked the heat from it. It laid siege for three days, appalling the newcomers huddled fearfully inside, awed by its fury and watching the drifts accumulate. It piled up on the hard-frozen ground and stayed until the Chinooks and the winds of spring lifted it and carried it away. When the storm moved on and the wind died, the temperature dropped like a stone, sending the mercury plummeting. Fingers of ice that had daily elongated from the shores finally touched and fused into bridges across the calm sections of the river. For a while longer the rapids talked, their soft liquid chatter heard in the still of the night. Then, they too froze over. After that, the only sound rising from the channel was the eerie booming of pressure ridges forming across it.

To Father and the Lowerys there was nothing unusual about the onset of this particular winter; to them it was about as normal as they came. They took the dry, searing cold as a matter of course. The Lowerys had been raised with it. Mother and the children, however, were unfamiliar with its bite and suffered because of it. As simple as a trip to the outhouse was, it became a hurried affair, followed by a hasty retreat to the house with stinging faces and hands and numbed parts that had come in contact with the wooden seat. They became reluctant to venture forth to the point of acute discomfort.

Nor were they equipped for it. Their clothing, although adequate to ward off the miserable dampness of the North Sea coast, was unsuited for the deadly cold of Alberta that could freeze unprotected skin in a matter of minutes. Young John was still wearing the short pants and blazer of the English schoolboy. Mother was better off than the children; she had brought two trunks of clothing with her. Being young and with only herself to worry about she had spent somewhat lavishly on clothing. The garments, wool and cashmere and bordering on luxurious, were warm and fashionable but not designed for life on an Alberta homestead. They did, however, provide protection if layered on one over the other. The children were not so fortunate; their mother had had to make her income stretch, and as a consequence, they had little more than what they stood up in.

Clothing themselves became critical and was one of the first things to be addressed. There was not a lot to be had in Sangudo. Albers' store that had opened in 1915, had clothing, but mostly for men and boys. Mother fingered the denim overalls and the heavy shirts, their fabrics unfamiliar to her touch. The very look of the wool underwear made her itch. Wearing it next to her body was unthinkable.

"Is there nothing for women to wear?" she asked. "Do women wear clothes like this? And girls—what do girls wear?"

"Some women wear overalls, and most girls do," said Mrs. Albers, a hardy woman who had arrived with her husband and two sons, having floated down the Pembina River on a raft to open the first trading post in the area.

"Do you not have woman's clothing . . . skirts . . . sweaters . . . you know . . . things that a woman or a girl can be seen in?"

"This is about all we have. Most women sew and they usually make their own clothes . . . either that or they send to Eaton's."

"I'm afraid we couldn't . . . you know. I'm sure English women don't wear clothing like this. We'll have to make do with what we have."

"We do have some cloth . . . in bolts . . . and thread, and things like that," said Mrs. Albers, sympathetic to this English woman whose tastes were different and who had not yet adjusted to the country.

There was cloth, but more decorative than practical—nothing to make warm clothing from.

"No. I'm afraid there is nothing here that we can use," said Mother. In her mind the thought still lingered that all she had to do was to walk into other shops along the street—shops that she would soon discover didn't exist.

They did outfit John from Albers', but for Nancy there was nothing. She was willing to wear boy's clothes—in fact, she was enthusiastic about doing so, but Mother was adamant. English girls didn't dress like boys. Instead, they dove into the trunks and adapted what was there. There was hesitation and a flood of tears as a beloved garment, a fashionable coat or skirt, fell to the scissors, but sadly there was little virtue in hoarding fashionable clothing; there was nowhere to wear it, and it seemed that there never would be. So they cut and sewed for hours on end, by hand, sitting at the kitchen table in the dim light of the coal-oil lamp. They, like most women of the time regardless of station or financial circumstance, had been taught the rudiments of sewing as young girls.

Father wore out his army clothing. He was not the exception; army uniforms had become the uniform of the homesteads. Returned soldiers as a matter of necessity and practicality wore what they had worn in the trenches. They wound the wool puttees around their calves, drew the balaclava helmets down over their ears, and then covered the breeches and tunics—many with sergeant's and corporal's chevrons still attached—with bib overalls and windbreakers.

They had a little money: Mother's savings and Father's accumulated army pay. Although not a spendthrift, Mother had not been one to save; there had been little incentive to do so thus far. Father had a few hundred dollars, a considerable amount for him. Being hospitalized for the best part of a year, he had not had the opportunity to squander it, as he would likely have done had he been physically undamaged. That and his separation allowance was what they had, and there was no further source of income.

There were many things to buy.

Their first major purchase was a team of shaggy-maned geldings, a black and a bay, named Paddy and Barney. These two names figured largely in my early vocabulary, being easy to get my tongue around. A homestead could not function without horses. These came with harness: an aged assortment of rusted buckles holding cracked, sweat-stained leather together. Earl Lowery sold them a sleigh, weathered and much repaired, but good enough to haul lumber and the materials to renovate the house. Father found a route down through the willows to the river—an easier one than they had used in desperation the night they arrived—and when the ice became thick enough to support the team, he crossed over and started work.

There was an urgency to get settled before the baby was born and also to relieve Lowerys of their uninvited guests, so he worked hard, as hard as his physical condition would permit. He made light of his earlier promises to Mother, feigning surprise that she had taken them seriously. In England they hadn't seemed too fanciful and it had been amusing to regale a young schoolteacher with the fictional description of his ranch. Now, the errant birds had come home to roost, and he felt compelled to prove that what he had portrayed was more than just a grandiose dream. He had to concede that at this stage, his ranch did not live up to its advance billing, but given time, by God, he would produce some semblance of what he had pledged. Mother, who watched him work, kept a stiff British upper lip, but suffered a painful knot of despair in her stomach.

He began by renovating the house. He removed the sod roof and added to the walls, raising them high enough to make a loft bedroom. There were horses now, and skidding logs was easier. Earl Lowery gave him a hand to lift them in place, and John although only ten was dragooned into helping, although under violent protest.

Father was not a skilled axeman and even had he been, hewing frozen poplar was risky—as many an old-timer, hobbling about on scarred feet, would attest. A razor-sharp axe glancing off frozen wood could amputate a toe or slice a foot or a leg in an instant, so he was careful, and the work went slowly. Mother followed its progress from the across the river. In the clear cold air, she could see the axe fall, and then a moment later, hear the solid 'chunk' as it hit the frozen wood. She watched the house rise, disappointment adding to her mountain of despair. It bore no resemblance to what she had envisioned.

He wasn't a skilled carpenter either. Building a gable roof, fitting windows and a door was, for him, a laborious cut-and-try process. He had few tools: a hand-saw, a hammer, a square and a wooden jack-plane. Learning to use them was also a cut-and-try process.

In the meantime, under the tutelage of Irma Lowery,

Mother and Nancy were learning the secrets of keeping house. In the cramped steamy space, they cooked, scrubbed clothes on a scrub-board, washed dishes and swept floors. Mother's hands that had never done anything more demanding than play the piano or hold a tennis racquet suffered. They became red and coarse from harsh soap and the cold. They were victims of frostbite time and again, as she hung clothes on the line and retrieved them frozen stiff. There were no hand lotions to assuage the damage.

Irma, a product of the country, was a marvel of patience. She had been raised without formal education, but had soaked up all of the domestic skills along the way as she grew up. To her there was no mystery about them; they were a normal part of becoming a woman. She was endlessly amazed at the awkwardness with which Mother and Nancy performed the simplest tasks, but she taught them, and they learned. They learned to put a meal together despite vegetables boiled to a pulp and meat either raw or charred. Mother learned to bake bread. There were more tears when her first efforts came out of the oven as hard bullets that even the dog scorned. But even baking bread came with practice. She had the will, and it became a matter of pride. If a backwoods person like Irma could do it, then an educated English woman could do it better. She did learn, but she would never be a good cook.

There would be no furniture, at least not of the kind that Mother had her heart set on. That came as another disappointment. There was no money for furniture; like the house, it would be made by Father. They did buy a stove, four wooden straight-backed kitchen chairs and four Winnipeg couches—iron cots that could be interlocked to make a double bed—covered with thin felt mattresses. All were second hand, bought by combing the country for whoever would sell them. Father made a kitchen table and benches to match from lumber left over from the house, brutish heavy things without a hint of grace to them. Wooden boxes, stacked and nailed to the wall, became cupboards. People gave them things like dishes, pots, and pans.

There was a time in the spring when the river could not be crossed; a time when the ice became too rotten to support the weight of a team and sleigh, and from then until the ice had been flushed from the channel by the melt. After that, the ferry a few miles downstream could be launched and vehicles could cross. Sometimes as long as a month would pass, depending on the weather, when the only access to Sangudo and groceries was by walking across the railroad trestle. Father calculated well. They crossed over, bringing all of their possessions with them at the last possible moment on the notoriously treacherous spring ice. It was a heartthrobbing, breath-holding crossing, with the water bubbling up around the sleigh runners and the horses wall-eyed and snorting, unsure of their footing and fully aware of the danger.

Now, they were on their own, cut off from Lowerys.

They left as friends and over the years would remain so, but there was also relief at no longer being dependent.

My sister Olwyn was born at the beginning of August after a hot humid spring and early summer in which the mosquitoes and blackflies came boiling out of the sloughs to make life a living hell for man and beast. There was no escape from them. It was either be eaten alive outside or suffocate inside. There were no screens for the door or windows and the heat from the wood stove, even just to boil the kettle for tea, turned the interior of the house into an oven.

Father had gone as far as he could with renovating the house and had turned to other things. He had started to build a barn for the horses and a cow and a house for chickens. He cut and skidded more logs from the flat land to the south, land that would become our first fields. They bought a cow, a matronly beast named Beauty who was pregnant and who they hoped would produce sufficient milk for a baby. As a parting gift, Lowerys gave them six hens, two of which were promptly eaten by coyotes.

He worked from daylight until dark by himself in the heat, battling the clouds of blackflies that hung over the him and the horses, drawn there by their sweat. They crawled into his ears and eyes and raised welts on his unprotected neck and face. He became thin and drawn. He had a haunted look in his eyes. His nerves were frayed and his temper flared with little provocation. For he and Mother, there was little of the romance that young couples could rightfully expect in the first few months of marriage.

Mother had her own problems. As her pregnancy advanced and her discomfort increased, irritability lay close to the surface. There was nowhere to get comfortable except to lie on their sagging bed. Keeping herself clean was almost impossible. As she became increasingly awkward, tears of frustration came readily. She cried at each mishap—of which there were many—as she attempted to prepare interesting meals from a limited larder as a token reward for Father's Herculean labour, wash clothes and keep them mended. Food spoiled because she cooked it badly or didn't know how to preserve it before or after it was cooked. The water, bailed up a bucketful at a time from the creek, teemed with insect larvae, wiggling creatures that had to be strained out before tea could be made or a drink taken. She had no one to turn to. Nancy and John were surly companions, out of their element and lonely.

She wanted to consult a doctor for no other reason than to talk to an educated person to discuss having a baby. She needed someone to reassure her that everything was as it should be. She had had scarce opportunity to talk to other women since leaving Lowerys.

The nearest doctor was Dr. Mann, at Robinson's Crossing. He had arrived there with the railroad. When it moved on, he stayed, but it wasn't a lucrative practice. Patching up damaged railroaders and the odd homesteader didn't pay much. Canada was dry at the time, and the only way that alcohol could be purchased was with a prescription from a medical practitioner. It was common knowledge that Dr.

Mann kept his head above water by issuing the right kind of prescriptions.

They made the trip to Robinson's in an aged wagon that Father had found abandoned and reclaimed. It was an outing if nothing else. Dr. Mann agreed that Mother was pregnant and opined that in due time she could expect a baby, but he offered little else in the way of a medical opinion. In the course of conversation, though, he suggested that Nancy come and visit them . . . stay with them for a few days. He and Mrs. Mann had no children and having a young person in the house would liven it for awhile. Mother and Father agreed to mull over the suggestion and eventually Nancy did go to visit them. Although of a sunnier disposition than John, Nancy was suffering from depression and loneliness and welcomed the opportunity.

John and Father didn't get along. John was a rebellious youth and Father a believer that the imposition of army discipline could quell any recalcitrance. The result was mostly open warfare. One day in a fit of temper at being told to chase the horses out of the small garden plot, John became over zealous and got too close. One of Paddy's huge unshod hooves caught him in the face, splitting his lip and breaking his nose. Father caught the horses and drove John to Robinson's where Dr. Mann stitched him up—without benefit of anaesthetic. He carried the scars throughout his life.

Mother went into labour in the early morning. Father hitched the horses to the wagon, loaded her aboard and headed for Robinson's Crossing, leaving Nancy and John to look after the farm. They must have been woefully ignorant or blissfully optimistic about the mechanics of birthing. They actually expected to travel three miles in a farm wagon (without springs), arrive at Robinson's in time to catch a train for Edmonton—a trip in excess of three hours—and then find their way to a hospital.

They miscalculated.

They got almost to Robinson's, then Olwyn became impatient

and began to make her appearance. Father swung the team into the nearest farmyard and stopped at the door of a low, dour-looking log house owned by Scotty and Liela McHardy. They were typical of the country and the time. They asked no questions, just rose to the occasion, helped Father get Mother inside and into their bed and dispatched Malcolm, the son, to fetch Dr. Mann. Malcolm might well have saved himself the trouble; Olwyn was born before he was out of the gate.

They stayed for three days. The house was infested with bedbugs, and Mother spent the whole time trying to keep the baby free of them. Father took them back to the homestead where Mother wouldn't enter the house until she had stripped herself and the baby, bathed both, and then boiled everything they had worn in a tub heated over an outdoor fire.

Ten months later, Mother was pregnant again. This time with me. I was born in early March 1921 after an endless winter. There was no thought of going to Edmonton this time; Robinson's and Dr. Mann would do. As luck would have it, Dr. Mann was away. McHardys had moved, as had most of the other residents of Robinson's. They cast about, looking for a house—any house inhabited by womenfolk. Smoke was issuing from the chimney of Gays' farm house, a half-mile west. Bill and Mrs. Gay and their married daughter Rena Johnson were all home and, like McHardys, they didn't ask questions; they just pitched in and did what was called for. I was born shortly thereafter. The Gays became grandparents to me. I called them Grandma and Grandpa until they left the country some years later.

Nancy went to live with Manns. What had started as visits for a few days lengthened until all thought of returning to the farm went by the board. Although Mother could have used the help, there really was no other reason for her to be there, and the house was becoming crowded.

By the fall of 1922, Father had taken off our first crop: three acres of oats cut with a scythe, the bundles tied by hand and stacked in a round stack—a complex interleaving of sheaves that wouldn't fall over and that could withstand downpours without the interior becoming wet. He had bought a plough and had broken sod on the flat, south of the house. He sowed it by broadcasting the seed by hand, in the same age-old method depicted by Francois Millet in his painting, *The Sower*. It was sinewy land, laced with poplar roots, that gave way reluctantly to the plough. Father had worked mightily for this small return.

The barn and the chicken house were complete and the garden protected with a pole fence. John had helped, but he and Father were increasingly at each other's throats. In mid-winter they had a falling out that culminated in John leaving. He crossed the river to Lowerys, lived with them until spring, and then moved on. He worked on farms, earning a dollar and his board wherever he could. He was fourteen. He came back once, four years later, and stayed the winter. He had matured to adulthood, and he and Father managed an uneasy truce. With the melting of the snow he again left, gravitating to Vancouver. He never returned.

By spring Father had cut more logs, and with a neighbour, Jim Clarke, imported a steam-powered portable mill and had them sawn into lumber. He used it, green as it was, to build a lean-to bedroom on the north side of the house. It was slightly smaller than the original log room, but the house suddenly took on a spaciousness.

My brother Owen was born in late February, 1923.

Mother went into labour in mid-morning. A young foot-loose English lad, Fred Finney, who had happened by and was staying with us for a few days, volunteered to go on foot for Dr. Mann. It seemed that they had given up taking Mother to him. Unfortunately, the doctor again missed out on the action; Owen arrived before Finney had gotten well on his way. Father added midwifery to his list of accomplishments.

A story went the rounds, passed on to any neighbour who would listen, that Finney successfully located Dr. Mann and returned with him, riding in his horse-drawn rig. Mann, I guess, somewhat miffed at again having missed the main event, was gruff. He demanded something to eat and twenty dollars for his trouble. Father complied, but never quite forgave him; it was the only money he had.

The Manns left shortly after, taking Nancy with them to California. Neither she nor they ever returned. Mother would never see Nancy again.

The farm had not reached the stage of producing a cash crop, except for eggs, but then everybody had eggs and the stores in Sangudo were glutted with them. By this time a second store had been opened by a man named McIvor. People said that his heart was too soft and often rather than refuse some destitute family he would take the eggs, give them a few groceries in return, and then as soon as they were out of the store, dump the eggs in the alley. He went bankrupt in a few years.

Father's health began to fail—not just his physical health, but his mental health as well. Too many things had crowded in on him. There was the constant worry of providing a living for Mother and three children. The work was hard and unending with precious little return. Relations between he and Mother were strained—she had her own set of problems. The outlook for farming was not at all rosy and he missed the free and easy life he had once enjoyed. More and more he thought about it. He got on the train and went to consult an army doctor in the veterans' hospital in Edmonton. The doctor poked and thumped, but finding nothing on the surface, wanted to probe deeper, perform a series of tests over a prolonged period. He hinted that Father might be entitled to a pension, although he didn't specify for what ailment.

He couldn't just walk away and leave Mother and three small children on the farm, so they sold the livestock and implements—they had some vague thought of giving up the homestead and remaining in the city—closed up the house and moved to Edmonton. We lived in Edmonton for the winter in destitute circumstances. I was two.

Nothing conclusive came of the tests. The following spring, Father borrowed two thousand dollars from the veterans' administration of the day and moved us all back to the farm. There were no jobs for which he was qualified in Edmonton. The pension would materialize, but not for a few more years.

We took up where we left off.

Another team of horses, Prince and Queen, replaced Paddy and Barney. A couple of cows, Daisy and Buttercup, replaced Beauty who had, during the desperate winter of 1922, become beef, and whose bleached skull adorned the gable of the chicken house for years. A few chickens multiplied into a vast flock. There were more farm implements and a rocking chair for the kitchen.

The work was no easier and Father's health was no better, but nevertheless he laboured. The bush receded and the fields broadened, but only by dint of unending toil.

Mother didn't do farm work but limited herself to the garden. Sometimes she would feed the chickens and gather eggs, but that was all. She wouldn't wear men's work clothes, as did the majority of farm women. She let it be known early on that she was a genteel English woman, a school teacher, and she didn't do field work or milk cows. Hers, to some degree, was the thinking that had been the downfall of many a Britisher in the wilderness, the kind of thinking that may even have been responsible for the Franklin expedition's disaster: a refusal to adapt comfortably to the country. Going native, they called it, and they shrank from any suggestion of it. She sank into a slough of depression and ill health; she gained weight, until at one stage she weighed close to two hundred pounds, but she didn't go native. She remained a genteel English woman, albeit dressed in flour sack dresses on which the label and printing could still be seen.

She ceased to communicate with her family in England. She couldn't bring herself to lie about her life, and the truth was something she didn't want known.

There were chores for children—even little children. As we became stable on our feet we naturally took on chores. My brother and I gradually became responsible for the feeding of chickens, terrified though we were of the two huge black roosters, Caiphas and Pontius Pilate, who ruled the flock and the barnyard for years. We milked cows, my sister and I, and we went into wooded pasture to search for them. We sawed firewood with a long two handled saw, hours on end. We worked in the garden and we helped Father break sod and the most hateful job of all, picking roots . . . hauling on the underpinnings of poplars, some of them fifteen feet long, and piling them for burning.

It wasn't all toil and trouble, though; there was recreation. There was swimming in the river and catching of fish that lurked in the eddies—huge pike that could take a fully-fledged mallard duckling from the surface with one gulp. There was tennis played of a summer evening—over the wire garden fence with wooden paddles and a nondescript ball—the rudiments learned there, the beginning of a lifetime of love for the game. There was singing. To Father, a Welshman, singing came as naturally as breathing—even in the depth of depression he sang. Mother, who was a musician and had had some voice training, sang to entertain us. We all sang. We sang in the evening before bedtime. We sang sitting in the sleigh on the way home from town or a visit to a neighbour, with a billion stars overhead and the jingle of trace chains for accompaniment. We sang hymns of a Sunday morning, miles from any church. We sang for the sheer joy of singing. It was the only music we knew.

There was isolation. There were illnesses never diagnosed. If we were sick we got better—in spite of some of the home remedies. After Dr. Mann left, there were no doctors nearer than Edmonton and taking a sick child to Edmonton to see a doctor was unheard of. A horse was a different matter. More than once, Father hastily boarded the train for Edmonton to consult a veterinarian about a sick horse.

Children, I guess, were renewable, horses were expensive.

There was despair, summer flies and mosquitoes, winter cold and the never ending work, but there was also love, the knitting together of a family that, despite individual frailties, remained as a unit. There was a bonding between siblings that grew stronger as the years passed.

We were not unique. We were a product of a time that was unique, a time at the end of a great war, a time when there were still vast tracts of land unsettled and to be had for the asking and a five dollar pre-emption fee. We were the settlers of that time.

4 • A Favourable Day

WE ARE GOING TO TOWN. THE DECISION NO LONGER SOMETHING to toy with has been made. We are out of groceries and we have to go.

It is always the need for groceries, the mail, some item of hardware or clothing that prompts us; seldom if ever for the sheer pleasure of going, what pleasure exists is offset by the tedium of the trip. It is an excursion never undertaken lightly.

The weather is finally favourable. Our going is always governed to some extent by the weather; its vagaries dictate who goes, or whether we go at all. Forecasting it is a sort of black art practised by Father. Whenever a trip to town is contemplated, he first studies the calendar for the moon phase, then he stands in the yard and gazes at the sky and the cloud formations. He notes the direction of the wind, and he searches for sun dogs—those rainbow-like sentinels on either side of the sun that he sets great store by. If he senses rain or snow in the offing and the need is not dire, he usually comes down on the side of postponement, sometimes for days. It depends on the degree of necessity. If it is absolute—something as critical as being out of tea or sugar or matches or oil for the lamps—and the clouds in the west look ominous, he goes by himself, prepared to face whatever might develop. If Mother has to go, occasioned by some purchase that only a woman can make, then by necessity we all go and a good day is essential. At times, a month will pass without there being a day favourable enough.

Provisioning and outfitting troops for some major skirmish is no more carefully planned than our trips to town. The well-being of five people, three being small children, for a long day of sitting in a wagon (or in winter, a sleigh) has to be carefully thought out. Winter blizzard or summer thunderstorm; it is the same. The worst has to be planned for. Our transportation is not the covered wagon of the American West nor that of the South African Trekboer that we can shelter in to ride out a downpour; ours is a simple farm wagon, wide open to the elements, drawn by the same heavy work horses that pull our plough and other farm implements, and the round trip to town is eighteen long, slow, jolting miles.

It is late March and the tail end of a stubborn winter that has hung on long after everyone is thoroughly sick of it. Snow squalls still regularly march out of the northwest, sometimes several in a day with tantalizing sunny breaks between. The temperature hovers barely above freezing, just high enough to keep snow from accumulating on the ground. Father has kept looking at the sky and has been putting things off for almost a week.

"Maybe tomorrow things will settle down," he has kept on saying.

"We can't wait much longer. We're out of just about everything and there's cream and eggs to take," Mother reminds him. "We'll just have to bundle up and pray for sunshine."

"I suppose so," he says. "And I guess we'll have to take the wagon. There won't be enough snow left on the road for sleighing. I'll have to get the box moved."

The semi-annual chore of moving the box—down from the wagon to the sleigh in the fall, and up from the sleigh to the wagon in the spring—cannot be avoided. Owning two boxes, one for each, is a luxury we can't afford. Moving the one we have would be simple for two people if Mother was more adept, but nothing in her background has prepared her for this kind of task and she is awkward at it. She can't figure things out, and she can't move easily or lift things. The result is that the box gets moved, but with shouting, bruised feelings, and periods of silence afterward. There are no mechanical aids and it is heavy. Strong as Father is, it taxes him to lift it, one end at a time, a few inches at a time, while shouting directions to Mother, who constructs a flimsy scaffold from poles and blocks to hold it. There is nothing we can do to help, except keep out from underfoot. My sister Olwyn keeps a tight reign on our three-year-old brother, Owen, and I bring a few blocks from the wood pile—but that is about all.

"Keep back, all of you. This whole thing could collapse," Father shouts, when the the box is finally high enough and blocked there. He and Mother cautiously tug the sleigh out from under the rickety structure and move the wagon into place.

Later, when the box is safely lowered and the scaffolding put away, I help with the greasing. I am given the can of grease to hold while Father scoops it out with a wood chip and smears it on the axles.

It is an old wagon, well-used when we got it. If it hadn't been, Father couldn't have afforded it; he'd had little money to buy a wagon or anything else when we came back to the farm in 1924. It was a good enough wagon when he found it, not a top-of-the-line one, but a serviceable wagon, and for what he intended—farm hauling—it had years of use left in it. There is no telling who made it; the carriage maker's brand has long since faded, weathered away in sun and rain, along with the last vestige of paint.

The wheels have grown thin from years of grinding contact with dirt and gravel roads, mud holes, and the bony ground of bush trails. They have worn to the point that the iron tires that encase them have become loose and during dry spells when the wood shrinks further, they come off. The cost of having them resized is more than we can afford, and even if there was money to do it, the question is always—is the rest of the wagon worth it. The answer—like the answer to a lot of farm repairs—is baling wire, or haywire as it is commonly called. Wrapped around the felloes between the spokes and twisted tight, it keeps the tires on but does nothing to enhance the appearance of the wagon. A bunch of extra lengths to replace the wraps that wear through bristles from the stanchion rings.

In age and appearance the box matches the running gear. Made from single wide boards bound together with carriage bolts and iron strapping, it has over the years contained most farm things to be hauled—bagged seed-grain, potatoes, livestock, and families like ours—winter and summer, on wagon or sleigh, for a long time. It has never known shelter, and it has weathered to a dull grey. The nuts, for want of a wrench to tighten them, have worked loose and some have dropped off. The bolts have backed out and been lost. The iron fittings are rusted and some are broken. The result is a box that flexes in every direction and squeaks in protest with every jolting turn of the wheels.

There were springs under the seat at one time, but they too have broken. The seat, now just a bench with a back on it, rests on the upper edges of the box. On no part of the entire rig is there anything to soften the jarring of the wheels. Every bump is transmitted directly to the tailbone of anyone sitting upright on the seat or in the bottom of the box.

It makes for noisy going: a cacophony of clopping hooves, squeaking wagon-box and clunking wheels on worn axles—a jarring, tooth-rattling orchestra of sound.

"A talking wagon pulls easy, and it's all we've got," Father had once said, summarizing its redeeming features.

"A bunch of Gypsies, that's what we look and sound like," Mother had commented, "except, I think Gypsy caravans make less noise, and they have springs under them. They certainly look better than our old wagon, that is, the last time I saw one it did."

Father has divined a reasonably decent day. The sky has

cleared, except for a few ragged clouds whose shadows like dark monsters course across the fields to the river and beyond. A stiff cold wind swirls scraps of straw in the barnyard and windrows them against buildings. Prince and Queen snort as Father leads them from the barn and the wind catches them, tossing their shaggy late-winter manes and tails. He hitches them to the wagon where they stand champing, ready to go. They are eager and will need holding in at first, but they will slow after a few miles. They are not carriage horses, and the boredom of plodding along the road for hours on end will take the starch out of them.

There is hay in the box. Covered with a horse blanket, it pads the bottom, taking a little of the shock from our undersides as we sit mile after jolting mile our backs propped against the side and rubbing against it. A second horse blanket is there to cover us.

In one back corner, tied down to prevent it wandering around, is the cream can. The five gallons of ripe cream is the product of our two cows over the preceding weeks. It has been saved in the can suspended deep in the well where the temperature remains constant—at this time of year, a few degrees above freezing. In the other corner is the egg crate wrapped in an old quilt. The lengthening days have prompted our motley collection of hens to prodigious output. Some dark brown; some speckled; some white. The eggs, varying from tiny to monstrous with two yolks, nestle in the cardboard dividers. The coal-oil can and an apple box with lunch in it ride in front under the seat.

Father boosts my brother into the straw-filled box. My sister climbs up a wheel, settles beside him on the horse blanket and pulls the other one over them. Mother, her weight making her ungainly, hoists herself up and onto the seat, grunting with the effort. I wait by the gate as Father climbs in and picks up the reins. The wagon rattles through and pauses. I close the gate and climb in. Judy, our border collie, sits at the top of the hill watching us depart.

The road snakes through the ravine where overhanging willows rake the sides of the box and reach inside for us. It continues across a pole bridge and up the other side. We can look back and see our buildings and fields. It is not a road that has been planned; it is the line of least resistance, carved out of the bush a little at a time, winding to avoid sidehills, rocks and stumps. It wanders through farms without any legal right to do so but tolerated for the time being until the day when the Government will build roads along the allowances between properties. It follows the river, past Clarkes,' close on the lip of the bank, to the old Holms' place, where only the brown-shingled windowless cabin is left standing. We can look down on the river where the ice is still fast to the shores, but is watery in the middle. Olneys' white house and their big log barn is across the fields to the left. Washing blows on the line, but there is no other sign of life.

The ground is still soft and the wheels roll almost quietly, although the clunking of the axles is always present. Down small declines where the horses trot a few paces, the haywire wraps on the wheels pick up mud and fling it high in the air to descend and settle on us. In the back, we cower under our horse blanket, but Mother and Father, sitting upright on the seat, are pelted with it. Father just hunches his shoulders and lets it slide off his denim jacket, but Mother is wearing her best coat, a black velour, and the mud sticks to it. She brushes at it, but until it is dry it won't come off. It is either mud or dust. When the roads are dry in mid-summer, dust comes boiling up and coats faces, clothing, and everything in the wagon.

We come to the ferry, a huge barge-like craft that is pulled up on shore. Later on after the ice goes out, it will be launched and we can cross on it, cutting the trip almost in half. But now we pass by, staying on the road that follows the river to the bridge downstream. We pass under the railroad bridge, a timbered structure more than a hundred feet high that spans the river and its valley. On the other side we can see the grain elevator and the railroad water tank towering above the rest of the town buildings. They look close, but it is another four miles before we get there.

Another mile and we join the Government road coming in from the north. It is hard packed and the noise level picks up and the ride becomes rougher. And then there is the bridge. The horses' hooves ring hollowly on the wooden decking as we cross.

We roll into town down the main street, past the barber shop, the two general stores and the hotel. It is noon time and we are hungry, but our first stop is the creamery. The cream has been churned for three hours over nine miles of country road. The sooner the creamery gets it the better. Father unties the can and heaves it out onto the loading dock.

"I hope it isn't butter," Mother says quietly.

Scotty McHardy comes out. He runs the creamery.

"Good day, Jack . . . Mrs. Jones," he says. "More cream, eh? Your cows must still be milking. The grade on your last can was pretty good—if I remember. You picked up your mail yet? Your cheque should be there."

"I hope it is," says Father. "We can use it."

Scotty yanks the lid off the can, takes a yellow pencil from behind his ear and dips the eraser end into the cream. He pulls it out and licks it.

"Not bad . . . ripe but not sour . . . pretty fair."

He lifts the can and carries it inside. He brings an empty one and drops it in the back of the wagon box.

"Thanks, Jack," He nods at Mother and disappears inside.

We drive across the railroad track and find a sunny slope out of the wind. Father unhitches the horses and ties them to the wagon box. They will eat the hay that has padded us. There will be little padding left for the homeward trip.

Mother spreads a horse blanket on the ground and unpacks the lunch: bread and butter, hard-boiled eggs and a quart of saskatoon berries. She has brought little fruit dishes to put them in, the ones we have saved from Quaker Oats and have too many of. We eat and then she brushes the mud from her coat. We walk up town carrying the eggs and the coal-oil can.

The post office yields up the cream cheque, along with a letter or two, Mcleod's machinery and hardware catalogue, and the *Grain Growers' Guide,* the magazine we subscribe to. We take the cheque, the crate of eggs and the coal-oil can to the general store. We move as a tight unit, Mother and Father in the lead and we three behind looking at everything, but fearful of straying far from them.

Father offers up the egg crate to Bert the grocer a thin, stick-like man wearing an eye shade and black cuffs over his shirt sleeves.

"The price of eggs has gone down," he says. "Everybody's chickens are laying again. I can give you ten cents a dozen— that's all."

He looks questioningly at Father and Mother. They nod. There is nothing to say. They have no bargaining lever. Father hands him the cream cheque and then takes out the grocery list. The cheque and what the eggs bring is what he will spend.

"Why don't you children go outside?" Mother says. "You don't have to stay with us. Go outside and find something to do."

There is nothing to do outside, but we go and stand outside the store, on the boardwalk and look. My sister hangs on to our young brother who would head off down the street if allowed.

There are a few people going about their business and the boardwalk rings with their boot heels. There are teams like ours tethered to hitching racks and fence posts, some still hitched to wagons. A wagon rolls past, drawn by a mismatched team, a big black stud-horse and a small brown gelding; it looks a lot like our wagon, and it makes the same noises. Clouds of sparrows come and go, seeking sustenance in the hay residue and horse manure under the hitching racks.

And there is an automobile. We stand, fascinated, looking

at it angle-parked in front of the store. It smells different from horses and wagons—a mixture of oil, gasoline, leather and hot metal—smells alien to our environment. We peek inside it and then back away hurriedly as a burly man comes purposefully toward it. He cranks it, gets in, and drives away leaving blue smoke and three overawed children behind.

We walk hesitantly along the sidewalk toward the garage where Charlie the owner is pumping gas. We watch the gas flow into the glass reservoir on top of the pump. Charlie is a bombastic little man with a protruding stomach. He is arguing and shouting at someone inside who is shouting back. It makes us nervous and we move on to look in the window of the drug store and then to Charlie Jones' harness shop. Mother comes out of the grocery store and walks toward the ladies' wear store at the end of the block. We fall in behind and follow her.

The ladies' wear is operated by Mrs. Thibert, a grey haired woman who seems to talk non-stop. There is little of interest for us to look at in her store, but there are chairs so we sit and wait while Mother and Mrs. Thibert talk.

"About all that woman peddles in that store is gossip," is Father's usual comment when Mrs. Thibert's is mentioned.

"Never mind. At least it's somewhere for me to go and talk to another woman," Mother says. "I don't get much opportunity to talk to other women, you know."

Mother urges us to go outside. My brother has fallen asleep in the chair, and my sister wants to look at the woman's magazines, so I go by myself across the street to the blacksmith's shop.

The blacksmith, a big man with dirt on his face, is turning the handle of his forge blower and whistling. He winks at me, a wink that tells me it is all right to stand and watch. Whatever he is making takes a lot of reheating. He pounds on it, making sparks fly in every direction and then jams it back in the fire. Every time he turns the blower he whistles. He finally takes a critical look at what he has been making and then plunges it into a water tank where it hisses and sends up a cloud of steam. He throws it on the floor with several more that look the same.

"Here, Sonny," He says and smiles at me. He hands me a small curiously formed piece of metal. I don't know what it is but I take it. I try to smile back at him, but I am too shy to say anything. I run back across the street clutching my prize.

Mother has bought something from Mrs. Thibert. She has a brown parcel in her hand. She says goodbye, and we troop out. She is smiling and her mind is elsewhere as we walk back to the grocery store. Mrs. Thibert has told her something intriguing. She pays little attention to us; we just follow along behind her. She keeps smiling and her mouth moves as though going over some of the conversation she has just had.

Father has hitched the team to the wagon and driven them to the front of the grocery store. He and Bert are loading the groceries. It is time to go home.

The road is no softer, and the horses have eaten most of the hay that padded us. The anticipation of seeing something different that enlivened us on the way to town is not there now. We know what lies ahead and boredom and the discomfort of being shaken by the wagon set in. My sister and brother and I didn't buy anything. There was no money for candy or ice cream—there never is. All I have as a memento is the curious piece of metal that the blacksmith gave me. I keep turning it in my hand and wondering what it is. Mother tells Father whatever it is that Mrs. Thibert has told her. She chatters away, almost like Mrs. Thibert—non-stop. Father's response is mostly grunts. He sits, slouched in the seat, the reins held loosely in his hand, swaying with the motion of the wagon. He was a professional teamster before he was a farmer and has ridden thousands of miles in wagons. He rides easily. It is still cold despite the sunshine, and we huddle under the horse blankets.

Across the bridge and back to the road along the river we go, the horses plodding wearily. The sorrel gelding Prince, a gentle monster of a horse, has learned how to fall asleep while walking. Father sees his head sinking lower and lower and flicks him on the rump with the end of the leather rein. He comes awake with a start, stumbles and then breaks into a trot for a few paces, dragging Queen along with him.

We pass Olneys'. The sun has swung westward and the wind at last is dying. We are coming to the old Holms' place, the empty cream can ringing musically as it bounces around. My brother, who has been half asleep for awhile, suddenly pushes the horse blanket to one side and stands up. He wobbles in the swaying wagon to the back of the seat and asks Mother to pick him up.

"No, no," she says, "you sit down. Be careful or you'll fall down. We'll be home pretty soon . . . not much longer now."

He begins to cry.

"Olwyn," she says. "Get him to sit down."

Olwyn reaches for him but he fights her. He lets go of the back of the seat and staggers around. He is wearing a red toque and a long scarf. The scarf comes undone and the end hangs over the side of the box. It gets hooked on the twisted end of one of the wire wraps on the front wheel. As the wheel turns, it yanks him out of the box. In a flash he is gone, hooked like a pike out of an eddy. I twist around and look over the side. He has landed on his back, all spread out and in an instant the big back wheel runs over the pom on his toque. Olwyn and I both shriek.

"Owen has fallen out!"

"Woah! Woah!" Father shouts and hauls on the reins. Before the horses have a chance to stop, he is down on the ground hurrying back to where Owen is lying. He squats down beside him. Owen just lies there. Mother climbs down a wheel. I have never seen her move so fast.

"Is he all right?" she asks. Her face is pale.

Owen begins to move.

"I think so," Father says. "He's got the wind knocked out of him, but that's about all."

Olwyn and I watch over the side of the wagon box. He is all right. He is a little stunned but doesn't seem to have broken anything. Mother picks him up and holds him tight. He begins to cry. Mother wipes his face and talks to him. There are tears on her face. Father gets back in the wagon and Mother passes Owen up to him. She crawls back up the wheel. They put Owen between them on the seat and Mother puts her arm around him. Father looks back at Olwyn and me and growls, "If you kids would just behave yourselves . . . ."

He chirps at the horses and we move on. Owen turns and looks back through the bars on the seat at Olwyn and me. He grins at us. He is where he wanted to be in the first place.

The horses trot a little, and our wagon talks.

It will be good to get home.

5 • The Trappings of Youth

T HE SNAG STOOD ON THE LIP OF THE BIG GULLY THAT RAN DOWN TO the river. It was an ancient snag, tall and brown, all that was left of a huge spruce that had outlived its genera-tion, and then itself succumbed, isolated from everything but its offspring: the waist high seedlings bristling at its base. Its top had blown away, leaving a long spear, like a yellow finger pointing at the Alberta sky. Woodpeckers had found it and drilled for grubs under its bark and hammered out nest holes that stared like sightless eyes from its rotting bole. The tail-ings from their probings formed a thick carpet below. Beneath this insulating mat, a colony of squirrels had settled in to winter in burrows excavated between the roots, their stored hazel nuts and seeds buried in the duff. About three feet from the ground a single skeletal branch protruded.

That's where I hung the chicken.

It was a skinny chicken, malformed and sickly. It should have died at birth, but it had hung on, growing to adolescence and then had its meagre warmth sucked from it by the first cold December night. Its claws, clamped and frozen to the roost, had kept it upright in the pack of healthy bodies around it. We had found it in the morning, and Mother had plucked its feathers, on the off chance that underneath there might be at least the makings of soup.

"It doesn't look very good, does it?" she said, scanning its wrinkled skin, holding it up to the light by the legs, its stringy body that had thawed in the warmth of the kitchen hanging limp and pale. "It may have tuberculosis. We had better not take a chance on it."

"I could use it for weasel bait," I said.

"Yes . . . you could do that. I don't think we should even feed it to the dog. Here, take it."

I took it, tied a string to its legs and carried it across the field. I walked in the narrow stock trail trampled in the snow past the straw stack to the snag. By the time I got there, it was frozen again.

The four traps nestled in the wood chips under the bulge of the trunk that kept them clear of snow were undisturbed. It was too cold for squirrels to be out. I tied the chicken to dangle a few inches above the ground. A hunting weasel, drawn by the scent of squirrel burrows, might be attracted to it and stumble into one of the traps while trying to reach it. I checked my fifth trap on the way home. It was in a hollow log that I had seen weasel tracks enter. It too was undisturbed.

I had been given the traps last summer by Old Man Wright, a tall, spare, old man with iron-grey hair and a kindly seamed face. He lived beside the river upstream from the ferry that he had operated until age had gotten the best of him and he had relinquished it to his son-in-law. Most people, young and old, referred to him as Old Man Wright. They called him Mr. Wright to his face, and a few like Father who had known him for a long time called him "Frank." He had lived in the same log house surrounded by garden since what seemed like forever. His wife had died years ago, and he had just continued on living there alone.

He was famous for his sourdough starter that he'd said had been going for more than thirty years—in a stone crock on a shelf in the warmth above the stove—and his skill at preparing a chicken for the pot. "Three minutes from the time he lays hands on that chicken; that's all it takes him." His son Lorne would say and chuckle.

"You're getting to be a good-sized lad," he'd said to me one day when we had stopped by to pick some of his rhubarb—another thing he was famous for. "How old are you now?"

"I'm eight," I said.

"Eight, eh! Yes. You are growing up . . . able to help your dad quite a bit now, eh, and I suppose you'll be running your own trapline come next winter."

"No. I don't think so," I said, squirming a bit. "I don't have any traps."

"No traps! A boy your age, and no traps? We'll have to fix that. Come with me." He led the way to the barn that housed his cow and his driving team.

"Somewhere in here . . . I seem to remember . . . " He searched the walls, moving bits of harness, bundles of twine severed from oat sheaves, gunny sacks and old horse blankets all covered with chaff and the dust of years. "Ah . . . here we are."

They clinked dully as he lifted them from the nail, a bundle of rusted, grimy traps—five of them.

"There now. There's a start for you." He handed them to me. I took them by the chains. My arm sagged with their weight. They were so old and rusty, I wondered if they would work.

"Them is Victor traps, size . . . number one, I think." He looked closely at them. "Yeah, number one, big enough to hold a weasel or a muskrat. There you are. Next winter you can start a trapline."

"Gee . . . thanks," I said. "I don't know how to set them, though."

"Here. Let me show you." He took one of the traps, set it on the ground and motioned to me. "Put your foot on the spring . . . right there. Now step on it. Hold it down. Now take this trigger over the top of the jaw and hook it in this notch in the plate. Now ease up. That'll do it. Now be careful you don't catch your fingers. There isn't much to it." He reached under the jaw, pressed the plate with his thumb and let the jaws clang shut. "There now . . . easy as pie."

I was all for setting them as soon as I got home.

"It's no good setting them now," Father said. "Even if you did catch something, the skin would be no good. You have to wait until it gets cold and the animals grow their winter fur . . . along toward the end of November. I'll let you know when."

I hung the traps in the barn and forgot about trapping; there were a lot of summer things to think about.

The November issue of the *Grain Growers' Guide* reminded me.

On the back page was a list of the going prices for fur for the coming winter. I pored over them for days with Mother helping me to decipher the animal names. The best price was for lynx: twenty dollars. I would trap a lynx.

"Those traps won't hold a lynx. You had better set your sights a little lower," said Father.

"OK, how about mink, or otter? I could catch them I bet. Look! fifteen dollars for a mink . . . "

"I think you better start with squirrels and weasels."

"Yeah but . . . only fifty cents for a squirrel."

The big snag could be seen from the house. It was just part of the landscape and I had never paid much attention to it. It caught my eye one day in late fall. There seemed to be squirrels all over it. They were hanging upside down, scolding and spitting at me as I passed on the way to get the cows. I bet that would be a good place to set a trap, I thought.

It turned cold, away down below zero, and snow came driving out of the northwest. The river went quiet, leaving the hissing of the wind across the stubble fields and the groaning of logs walls as the only night sounds. The coats of the animals were sleek and heavy and the dog could stay in the house only a few minutes before she began to pant with the heat. It was time to set the traps.

"I'm not an expert trapper, but I know something about it," Father said. "I'll go with you . . . help you to set the traps the first time . . . if you want."

"OK . . . I guess, but I want to do it."

It was a cold, crackling morning with the sun low and shining in our eyes. I carried a hatchet in one hand and the traps in the other. They made a hard, metallic sound, rattling on the end of their chains. I felt important as I walked beside Father's stocky denim-clad figure; I was going to be a trapper. We scuffed through six inches of fresh snow across the field to the snag.

"We'll set four of them here, right on their doorstep," he said, raking the wood chips to one side with the side of his boot. "The other one . . . we'll find a place for it . . . maybe some place to catch a weasel."

"Let me set them; I know how. Mr. Wright showed me."

"Go ahead then, but be careful you don't catch your fingers."

It wasn't as easy as it had been in Mr. Wright's yard, but I got them all set and nestled in the burrow entrances. To my eye, they looked deadly, ready to reach right out and grab a passing squirrel. I pounded the chain nails into the base of the stump with the back of my hatchet. Now all I had to do was wait.

The relationship between a live squirrel, its tail perked up, its eyes bright and chattering cheekily at me and the price for its hide as listed on the back page of the *Grain Growers' Guide*, was something I hadn't dwelt on. I hadn't considered the necessity of killing an animal to get its pelt; all I could think of was the fifty cents it would bring. And I guess being able to call myself a trapper had a certain ring to it.

Nothing happened for the next couple of weeks. The cold deepened and the small things in the bush stayed quiet, nestled underground. I went regularly for a look, first thing in the morning and again late in the afternoon, walking on the lumps of frozen cow and horse manure in the stock trail, past the straw stacks and the cattle, hump-backed in the cold. Nothing at the snag had changed. We had set the fifth trap in a hollow log where a weasel track had entered, but it too waited with its jaws agape, undisturbed. Trapping, I began to realize, was a lot like fishing. The creatures I was trying to catch had to co-operate. I got a little discouraged.

A week after I hung the chicken up, there was a weasel in a trap, but not under the chicken. The trap in the log had caught it. It was a small weasel, barely six inches from its nose to the black tip on its tail. Its whole body was in the trap and it was frozen. Its lips were drawn back in a grimace; its tiny teeth clenched, testimony to the agony of its dying. It had suffered a slow and painful death, alone in the hollow log. A last spring's kit, it was less than a year old. I got a tight feeling in my throat. I was sorry I had caught it. I pried it out from between the jaws and shoved it in my coat pocket, a feather-light wisp of fur.

I reset the trap, unsure if I wanted to catch anything else in it.

"That's not much of a weasel," Father said, examining it. "A skin that size isn't going to make you rich."

"Yeah, it's pretty little. How do you skin it when it's frozen?"

"You'll have to let it thaw first. Take it in the house. I'll show you how to skin this one but from here on, if you're going to be a trapper, you'll have to do your own skinning."

After supper in the coal-oil lamp-lit kitchen, I laid newspaper on the table while Father whetted his pocket knife on a spit stone. He turned the now limp body on its back, slit the skin down the inside of its hind legs and began separating it from them with small strokes of his knife. A musky, wild smell came from it as he peeled the skin—inside-out—from the tiny blood-red body, scarcely as big as my finger. It looked ashamedly naked in the lamplight.

He whittled a pointed stretcher from a piece of box wood, hardly more than a splinter, and drew the little skin over it.

"It'll have to dry for a few days before you take it off," he said.

"When can I sell it?"

"Oh . . . next spring sometime. You'll probably get a few

more this winter. You can take them all at once."

Between Christmas and New Year's, a Chinook blew in for a day, settling the snow and bringing the woodland population above ground. There were tracks everywhere.

I heard the rattling of a trap chain while I was still a distance away. I wasn't prepared for the violence and panic at the base of the snag as I cautiously rounded it. A squirrel was in a trap and it was still alive, terrified and probably in pain. When it saw me it tried desperately to run up the trunk, but its hind legs were caught, and its front claws couldn't lift the weight of the trap. It fell back, turning over and over, biting at the jaws that imprisoned it. I didn't know what to do. Letting it go flashed through my mind, but I thought it might bite me if I tried to get my hands on the trap to release it. I didn't want to look at it; its struggles terrified me. In desperation, I grabbed a dead branch and hit at it. The wood was rotten and it broke. I found a bigger one and, trying not to look, I beat blindly at the writhing bundle of fur and steel until it became quiet.

I watched it for a few minutes. I had never killed anything before and I didn't like what I felt. I probed at it with the toe of my rubber boot. It didn't move. I put my foot on the trap spring and depressed it; the lacerated legs fell limply from the jaws. There was blood around its head and one eye had popped out of its socket. I felt sick. There was a lump in my throat and I wanted to cry. I picked it up and smoothed its fur with my fingers. I was surprised at the warmth of its small body.

I sat down on the sawdust layer, suddenly weak-kneed. I held the squirrel on my lap, smoothing its fur as its body began to stiffen.

I reset the trap, not because of any desire to catch more squirrels but because I knew Father would expect me to and started for home. It was warm enough to go bare-handed, and I carried the small body dangling by its hind legs. I felt a crawling on my hand; it was covered with lice. They were leaving their dead host for the warmth of my hand. I dropped it and brushed frantically at the tiny parasites advancing up my wrist. I tied a string to it and dragged it the rest of the way home, hoping the lice would be left behind in the snow.

Watching Father skin the weasel was one thing. Skinning a squirrel myself was something else. Father loaned me his sharp pocket knife, but sharp as it was, I had difficulty in cutting into the inside of the hind legs as he had done. The skin was unbelievably tough and the body so stiff I couldn't control it. The gamey smell as I finally drew the skin off was sickening. It had a few holes in it where the knife had pierced it, and there were bruises where I had hit it with the stick. It was tattered looking—hardly a prime pelt. It took me a long time to make a stretcher the right size and get the skin pulled on and tacked down. Afterward, I washed and washed, but even the scent of strong soap couldn't mask the smell of squirrel on my hands.

The cold descended again, deeper than ever. The chicken hung on its string, white and desiccated. It wasn't very appetizing looking, even for a weasel. I visited the snag daily.

"You have to look at those traps," Father was adamant about that. "You can't let an animal suffer because you think it's too cold to go and look."

I crossed the field hunched against the wind, my fingers and toes numb with cold and the lobes of my ears freezing, always hoping there would be nothing in the traps. I would stop and listen for the sounds of a rattling chain. Without consciously thinking about it, I knew if I heard it I would turn and leave, even though I knew it would be wrong to do so.

Being a trapper had its drawbacks, I decided.

A mild day at the beginning of February brought renewed activity. One trap was sprung and upside down. As I pressed down on the spring and opened the jaws to reset it, a small foot fell out. I had been told that animals would sacrifice a foot for freedom. They would actually amputate it by gnawing through skin and bone. That little foot, with its tiny pads, looked pathetic lying there in the sawdust.

My sister Olwyn, two years older than me, was probably of a better temperament to be a trapper than I. She was a tough-minded girl who had guarded me, but also bossed me unmercifully ever since I had taken my first hesitant steps. She was with me the day the big weasel was caught. I don't know how I would have reacted had she not been there.

We heard the rattling of the trap chain a long way off.

"Hey! there's something in a trap. C'mon, there's something caught." She hurried forward. I lagged behind hoping that whatever it was would escape.

"Golly! It's a weasel, a big one."

It was a weasel, all right, and a truly gigantic one. It was not cowed by its predicament or by the pain it must have been in. It attacked—straight at us—coming up short against the chain, but still striving to reach us, its lips drawn back in an intimidating snarl.

"You better kill it. Hit it with something," my sister said.

"It'll bite me if I get too close. You kill it."

"Come on. Kill the thing. It's your trap. What kind of a trapper are you anyway?"

"I don't want to kill it. Let's let it go."

"Let it go! We can't do that; it's worth a lot of money. Look how big it is. Just hit it on the head."

"I don't want to."

The weasel made an attempt to climb the snag. It stretched itself against the trunk. It was powerful and it lifted the trap to the full length of the chain. Without another word, my sister reached out from behind, grasped it around the neck with her thumb and forefinger, and choked it.

"Here, open the trap and let its leg out. I'm taking it home. Dad will know how to kill it."

"Its gonna bite you, I bet."

"It can't bite me as long as I keep a hold on its neck. Get the trap off it."

I squeezed the spring and its leg slipped from the jaws. She marched off, holding the squirming weasel out in front of her.

We were about half way home when she said, "My hand is getting tired. Here you hold it for awhile."

"I can't . . . without it biting me."

I had a piece of cord in my pocket. I took it out and tied its hind legs together.

"Now you can let it go," I said.

She released it. It immediately tried to escape, but I hung on to the string and reeled it back in. It turned and attacked me.

"Look out! It's going to get you," Olwyn shouted, half laughing as I jumped out of the way.

I dropped the string and ran. She grabbed for it and gave it a jerk, bringing the weasel up short. It tried to escape again. It clawed at the crusted snow with its front feet. She calmly reached out and grasped its neck again.

"Come on. Let's get it home."

Father's jaw fell when he saw us.

"Be careful! That thing could bite you, make a mess of your hand. What are you doing with it anyway?"

"We didn't know how to kill it so we brought it home. Can you kill it?"

He took the end of the string that was trailing from it.

"Let go of it."

He carried it over to the wood pile, it trying to climb up the string to get at him. I didn't watch.

"Here." He handed it to me. It had blood dripping from its nose, leaving a trail of bright red dots in the snow. The life and savagery gone, it was now just a slack, white, elongated bundle sagging from the end of the string.

"I think you better skin the weasel," I said to Father that evening. "I might not do it so good and I might make a mess of the skin."

"All right, I'll do it, but you watch. I'd say no, but it should bring a couple of dollars if it's done right."

I watched, becoming more convinced than ever that I didn't want to continue as a trapper.

The chicken disappeared the following week. There were coyote tracks around, and three traps were sprung. It looked like a big old dog coyote had stumbled into them as he was stealing the chicken. They probably did little more than pinch his toes.

I caught one more squirrel before the weather became too mild. It was dead in the trap, saving me making a decision. I skinned it and did a somewhat better job of it this time.

The river awoke. We heard it start about noon one day in April. There was a great grinding and shattering as the ice heaved and started on its way. We watched it go from the top of the bank, slabs of ice twisting and turning, nudging each other up onto the beaches. On the larger floes was a winter's history passing in front of us: animal tracks, the remains of hay stacks, winter roads, scraps of deer hide left from coyote kills, skating rinks, watering holes and a rowboat that hadn't been pulled up high enough last fall. It was a grand sight, this sudden unleashing of energy arrested by the winter. By the following morning the channel was clear, but running full and muddy. A few ice floes remained to melt where they had been stranded high above the stream.

"I think we better take those traps of yours and see if we can catch a few muskrats while their pelts are still prime," Father said, a couple of days later.

"I don't know how to catch a muskrat," I said, hoping to discourage him. I had never even seen a muskrat up close. I had seen the black dots of their heads and the trailing Vs moving across the calm eddies on quiet summer evenings, but that's as close as I had ever come to a muskrat.

"I'll show you," he said. "Rats are a good price this spring. A good one can bring as much as a dollar."

We took the traps away from the snag and threaded our way down the gully to the river. The silty beaches were soft and littered with driftwood and ice. Deer tracks were everywhere, and the child-like footprints of a porcupine ambled along under the overhanging willows. Down in here, the air was heavy with the dank smell of wet earth and the newly awakened river. The muddy water swished and sighed as it hurried past, rippling and scouring the soft banks. An occasional tree, roots pointing skyward, floated out in the mainstream. By midsummer the breadth would shrink by half, and the flow would become slow and clear.

"The water is too high to get at their dens," Father said, "I guess we'll have to set them on floats."

"How do you make a float?" I asked. I didn't really care how a float was made, but I thought I should ask. I was more interested in walking beside the swirling current and looking at what was written in the sand.

"I'll show you. All we need is a few short lengths of log."

We sorted through the driftwood, selecting flattish pieces. Father fixed them up with the axe, hewing places on them big enough to hold a trap and a few rounds of carrot that he had brought for bait. He moored them close to the shore with baling wire, tied to stakes pounded into the beach. We set all five traps in small eddies, clear of the main current, over a quarter mile stretch of river.

That evening there were two muskrats caught. They had pulled themselves onto the floats, gotten caught and fallen back into the water, taking the moored trap with them. The weight of the trap had held them under until they drowned. At least we didn't have to kill them.

The following morning, the ground was white again. As a last reminder, winter had dumped an inch of snow on us. We didn't go to visit the traps until late morning. By then the sun was warm, and the melt was well underway. As we exited the gully onto the beach, we intersected a set of tracks following the river, coming from up around the hogback somewhere. Made by the boots of a big heavy man, they were imprinted deeply into the snow and the underlying silt. The left foot was splayed to the side. Someone with a bad leg had walked this way.

The snow was trampled and scuffed where the first trap had been moored. The float was lying up on the beach, still tied to the stake, but the trap was gone. The nail holding the chain to the float had been pried from the wood.

"Somebody's deliberately taken a trap," Father said. "No animal could pull it off the float like that. Somebody's stolen it."

"That's my trap, one that Mr. Wright gave me. They can't just take it. That's stealing!" I said.

"That's what it seems like, all right," said Father.

We followed the tracks downstream. Each trap site had received the same treatment, and every trap was gone. The tracks continued, following the shoreline, and beside them in the snow were the marks of dirty water dripping from a bundle of traps—and maybe a few drowned muskrats—swinging from the hand of a thief.

"Now who in hell would steal traps?" Father said, incredulously, looking at the last beached float and the tracks continuing from it, marching on down the snow-covered sand. Stealing in our part of the country where nothing was ever locked was unheard of.

"I'm going to follow him, whoever he is, and see where he goes. Do you want to come or do you want to go home? We might have to walk a long way."

"I'll come," I said. I was curious and also a little fearful at the look on Father's face.

That the traps had been stolen was almost unbelievable, but when it finally hit me that they were actually gone, the first secret thought that went racing through my mind was one of relief: I wouldn't have to kill or skin anything else.

Whoever it was wasn't in a hurry. The length of stride hadn't changed. The tracks stopped at other likely places where traps might be set and then continued downstream. It was kind of exciting. I had never known of anything to be stolen before, and I had never been this close to a known thief. I followed Father, hard pressed to stay with him. He looked grim, and purposeful.

Another quarter of a mile and the tracks left the river

and climbed up a narrow path to the bench above. On top, the snow was melting in the sun and the tracks were becoming indistinct. By the time they joined the road, they were gone.

"I don't know who he is, but I'll know those tracks if I ever see them again," Father said. "It's got to be somebody local, and anybody who leaves tracks like that probably limps or walks strangely. I'm going to be on the lookout for anyone with a bad leg."

"Maybe we should tell the police," I suggested.

"Trouble is, the closest policeman is in Edmonton. It could be months before he comes this way. No. I'll find him. He can't live far from here."

We turned for home, walking side by side along the road.

"It's too bad you lost your traps. Maybe next year we could buy a few more . . . we'll see," Father said. He put his hand on my shoulder and pulled me over to him. He surprised me; it was about as close to a comforting gesture as I had ever had from him. I looked as solemn as I could, but inside I was glad.

The next time we went to town, we took the skins. Fred Hurt, the clerk in the Keely's store, was also the fur buyer for the district. I took my winter's catch from the cloth sugar sack and laid it on the counter. I tried to arrange them so the places where I had nicked them with the knife would be less obvious. Father stayed in the background, making like he was interested in horse collars and harness. Before we came into the store, he had said, "You have to stand on your own two feet. Make the best deal you can."

Fred looked at the skins. He didn't miss the knicks and tears. He turned them over and flexed them to see how dry they were. They crackled in his hands.

"Fur is not worth as much as we thought it was going to be," he started by saying. "The bottom fell out of the market."

"The prices were all in the *Grain Growers' Guide*," I said. "Fifty cents for a squirrel."

"Yeah . . . but those are for prime pelts. Look at these. They're kind of hard done by."

"Only one. The others are OK."

He hummed and hawed, as though his whole future depended on the decision he would make in the next few minutes.

"I'll tell you what; I'll give you a dollar for the big weasel and seventy-five cents each for the muskrats. The two squirrels . . . I don't know . . . maybe two bits for both . . . yeah . . . two bits. That little weasel . . . Gosh it's little. Did you take it away from its mother?" He turned it over.

"I'll give you four cents for it."

"Is that all?"

"Yeah . . . that's all . . . the best I can do. Like I said, the bottom fell out of the fur market."

He was a tall man and skinny. He looked down at me from his great height. I didn't know how to bargain with him. I had been brought up to believe that what adults said was not to be questioned.

"OK, I guess," was what I said, after a pause in which I tried to look as though I was considering several options.

He swept up the skins and carried them into the warehouse, then he opened the till and handed me some money. It was the most money I had ever held in my hand all at once. I didn't count it; I just handed it to Father. He and Fred looked over top of me and smiled at each other. Adults seemed to understand things that weren't spoken. There were things they weren't telling me, but I didn't really care. There was nothing I wanted to buy anyway; it was still too cold to go to Ernie's drug store for ice cream.

I didn't go to the snag any more. I passed close to it during the summer on the way to hoe potatoes in our south field, and sometimes I imagined I heard a trap chain rattle. One day in late September, a squirrel scooted across the path in front of me, heading toward the snag. I followed him out of curiosity to see if squirrels still lived under its roots. He ran up the trunk and hung there upside down, spitting and chattering at me, giving me what for. I guess I had it coming; he had only three feet.

6 • October Burning

WE BECAME AWARE OF THE SMOKE GRADUALLY. AT FIRST IT was just a metallic taste on the tongue. Then noticeably, the sky darkened and the clear blue that had been over us for weeks took on a soiled look. In the late afternoon the air was dull and heavy, unlivened by even the whisper of a breeze. It stung my nostrils and made my throat rasp. When I took a deep breath my chest felt tight like I was getting the flu or something. I moped around without much interest in anything, even eating. I was usually front and centre for that, but the prospect of supper didn't hold as much interest as it usually did. When the sun sank below the pasture fence, it left a huge dirty bruise across the western horizon.

That night in the close confines of the attic bedroom that I shared with my brother and sister, there seemed less air than usual. I got out of bed and spent a long time at the screened window, searching for a breath of normal night air with the good clean scent of hay and farm animals in it. In the morning, we all awoke feeling stuffy and listless.

As the day wore on, there was an oppressive feeling. Something was about to happen. No one said anything, but we felt it. We were all tight and irritable. More and more I saw Father glance at the sky from where we were working on the binder, cleaning and oiling it after the harvest. Even Judy, our border collie, was on edge, hanging around almost underfoot instead of making her usual patrols of the buildings, herding the chickens or sniffing out mice under the stooks.

As the afternoon waned, the sun hung red, a Cyclops eye in the west, bathing the buildings and stubble fields in an eery bronze glow: a strange light in which nothing cast a shadow.

I heard Mother talking to herself as she took the clothes from the line. She held the pieces at arm's length and then shook them vigorously.

"There's something all over the clothes," she called to Father. "Where do you suppose it's coming from?"

"It's probably ash drifting in from the fire," he replied. "It's a pretty big one by the look of it . . . somewhere back in the foothills, maybe closer. I don't know. Hard to tell where it is, or if it's coming this way. There's not much wind."

"Well, I hope it isn't. It's getting everything dirty, and it's awfully dry."

The cows came home early that evening. They came without my sister and I having to go for them, and their breathing was more laboured than usual as they climbed the hill from the creek. After milking they hung around the barnyard instead of wandering back to graze for the night. I had to chase them out to the pasture and close the gate to keep them there. The horses snorted and blew, as my brother and I took them down to the creek for water, testing the air and not liking what they smelled. They gazed around uneasily as we led them back to the barn.

I awoke several times in the night and looked out the window. The sky was lit with a dull red glow, and the smoke was thicker than ever. I heard Father moving around downstairs. He coughed, and then I heard him go out. I followed him. He was standing at the top of the hill overlooking the creek, facing northwest, his short broad figure motionless in the darkness.

"It looks like a really big fire," I said. "The smoke is sure thick."

"Yeah, and it looks like it's moving this way. There's not much wind behind it, but it's coming. I'm sure of it."

"How far away is it, do you think?"

"Hard to tell. Maybe five or six miles. It might stay north of us unless the wind changes."

"Do you think our house might burn?"

"Let's hope not. If it does spread this way, the creek might stop it." We stood there for awhile just looking at the glow in the sky, and then he said, "You had better go back to bed; we might have a busy day tomorrow."

I stood for a while longer, looking around at our farm buildings, at the huge shadow of the barn that bulked bigger than ever in the night, the smaller outlines of the house and squat outbuildings. They were rough, fashioned from logs, unpainted and weathered, but they were home. I had never known anything else but these buildings; they represented security. It was hard to believe they could disappear. I had seen the remains of burned houses with twisted bed springs sticking out of the ash and shattered precious possessions lying defiled by heat and smoke. I visualized our house burning and I felt scared—it wouldn't burn, not if I could help it, it wouldn't.

It was quiet. The distance was still too great to hear the roar and crackle of the fire. There was just the red glow playing silently in the sky. The only sounds were the quiet night stirrings I was used to: the horses bumping around in the barn, the sleepy cooing from the hen house, and the liquid sound of the river hurrying over its stony bed.

I went back to bed, but stayed awake for a long time, worrying.

Shortly after breakfast, a figure appeared, wraithlike, through the smoke that the night air had pressed down over the fields, striding down the hill and cutting across the stubble. I recognized the tattered appearance of Will Sherrett, our bachelor neighbour to the west. We watched him come, walking heavily and bent under a bulging pack sack. He eased it off his shoulders at the garden gate and dropped his hat on top of it.

"Good morning, Billy," said Father. "How does it look from your place?" There was no need to explain what he was talking about, the smoke did that.

"Good morning Jack . . . Paul," he said, winking at me. "It doesn't look good. It's in the muskeg north of Astles,' and it came south a bit. They plowed up a fire break, but not in time. They've lost their barn and some outbuildings. They managed to save the house, though."

"What about your place?"

"It's north of my line, as long as the wind doesn't change, I think it will miss my place. If my shack burns, there's not much loss," he said, with a wry smile. "Anything of any value, I've got with me, here in the pack." He nudged the bloated brown canvas with his toe. "It can have the rest of it. I thought you might need a hand. It seems it's coming this way."

"Thanks, Billy. That's good of you. We'll probably need all the help we can get. I don't know what we can do, though."

It was typical of Will Sherrett to show up now when he thought we might need help. That's the kind of man he was.

Even standing there in the smoke, in his torn shirt, bib overalls with holes in the knees and run-over boots, there was a dignity about him. And now, as usual, he had a smile on his hawkish face.

I didn't think there was a whole lot we could do, but we had to try. I felt good about having Will there. He would help us.

There hadn't been any rain for weeks, and the shingles on the house and the boards on the barn roof were tinder dry, bleached silver and curling. Any kind of a spark and the old log structures would go up like Roman candles.

"Water, as much of it as we can get. Fill everything," Will said. "That's how Astles saved their house, by keeping the roof wet. I'll give you a hand. Come on, Paul, let's carry water."

We collected every container we could lay hands on. The rain barrel was the biggest but because it had been empty so long, the staves had shrunk and it leaked like a sieve. We carried pailful after pailful from the creek, barely staying ahead of the leaks. It began to soak up, and we gained on it after an hour or so. We didn't have much else that would hold water, a few buckets and the washtubs. We put a washtub on the roof of the lean-to bedroom and filled it, Will, on the roof, pulling up the buckets with a rope, me and my brother carrying them from the creek. My brother was only eight, and he couldn't carry much at a time, but he worked hard. We both laboured in the smoky air, climbing the hill from the creek.

The barn roof was too steep to set anything on, so Father banged together a platform on the peak, big enough to hold our copper-bottomed wash boiler. He first had to make a ladder to get up there, a rickety affair, from small poles and scrap lumber. It was pretty high to the ridge pole, and he teetered there, pulling up buckets and walking along to empty them into the boiler. One slip and he would have shot down the sheer incline to the sloping ground below, breaking something or killing himself in the process. His worn leather-soled boots gave him little purchase on the smooth boards.

By now, the sun was high, the night's dampness had been lifted from the undergrowth, and the fire had picked up its pace. We could hear it, and great plumes of smoke were boiling up at the end of Jim Clarke's field across the line fence on the north side of the creek. It was terrifying. Despite there being little wind, it seemed to be advancing at an alarming rate. Nothing we could do was going to stop that fire—I knew it. The inclination was to run from it into clean air, anywhere where we could breathe freely again, but we had to stay and at least try to save the buildings. If the worst happened and we couldn't, then we might have to run.

Father harnessed the horses, hitched them to the wagon and drove them to the side of the house by the garden. They didn't like the smoke and the nearness of fire and were hard to handle, needing a firm hand on the reins. He tied them to the fence where they stood fidgeting and pawing the ground. Mother and my sister began loading essentials—bedding, dishes and food—into the wagon box. Mother was gasping from the smoke and exertion. Her face was scarlet and she was perspiring. I was afraid she would collapse. My sister, a strong practical type, took charge of packing things and carrying them to the wagon. She was only twelve, but she knew what to do and went ahead and did it.

I don't know where we planned to go, or if there was a plan at all. Our farm was at the end of the only road, and the fire would soon cut that off. We might go south, across the fields and the brushy benchland, down to the river and find a place to ford it. It wouldn't be easy but it had been done, a long time ago.

We opened the gate and let the cows into the south fields. From there with no fences to stop them, they could wander for miles if they felt like it. It was unlikely that they would cross the river, and they would come back eventually.

We closed the door to keep our old brood sow out of the sty. She had a couple of acres devoid of growth in which to run. She would be all right. She could flop into one the multitude of huge holes she had rooted up in the hillside. The cool earth would protect her. The chickens would have to fend for themselves. They were scattered throughout the fields that bordered the farmyard, picking up loose grain between the stooks. There was only a remote chance that our fields would catch fire.

The falling ash was hot now. It stung when it landed on exposed flesh. None of the sparks were big enough to start anything burning, but it would happen soon. Father and Will climbed up to the roofs and began throwing water around. My brother and I replenished it from the creek.

Wild things, those with the mobility to escape, began emerging from the brush. Prairie chickens took to the air, their wings drumming low over the stubble. Three deer trotted out and came towards us, following along the wire of the line fence. They passed directly in front of us a few yards away, paying us scant attention, intent only on escape. A mother coyote and a spring pup all ears and bushy tail, eased into the field and slipped quietly across it. All were heading east, following the creek to the river and safety. Our dog, who would normally have set up a loud hullabaloo and given token chase, was silent, watching them pass. Through some means of communication known only to them, they had established a truce; nobody was going to harass anybody at this time of common danger. I knew that in that maelstrom of fire and smoke there were others perishing: small burrowing animals, little birds, snakes and frogs, unable to move quickly enough, were being cremated. I heard keening sounds from the depth of the flames, and imagined them to be the voices of dying creatures.

The fire reached the stubble and was creeping across it, fanned by the winds of its own creating. It would slow, move from stalk to stalk and then flare up when it encountered a patch of compact straw pressed down by the binder's bull-wheel. It was hard to tell how broad the front was. It was raging in the bush north of the field, incinerating everything in its path. This was short timber country. The trees were compact and growing close together. I saw spruce trees, cone encrusted and rich in pitch, suddenly explode and become fireballs, their tops flying off and rolling ahead.

There was still no great wind, just that generated by the blaze and a light movement of air from the west that was keeping it moving east toward the river where it would stall.

Will came down from the house roof and helped my sister to climb up. The house was not as close to the fire as the barn, and fewer sparks hot enough to start the shingles burning made it to the roof. She could scramble around in her rubber-soled shoes and douse them with dippers full of water from the tub. He would help carry water for awhile. Father was still patrolling the barn roof pouring water down the steep pitch of the side closest to the fire. It took a lot of water and we were hard pressed to keep enough coming up to replace it. My brother was getting tired. The bucket was big and he couldn't carry much in it. He was only a little guy, and he had made a lot of trips to the creek. He started to cry.

"What's the matter with you?" I asked, not very kindly.

"Something's biting my back," he said, squirming and hollering.

I looked where he was trying to reach. He had his arm cranked around behind him, straining up between his shoulders. He was dancing around. There was a wisp of smoke rising from a red rimmed hole in his checkered shirt. He was on fire where a spark had landed. Without thinking much about it, I let fly with my bucket of water, dousing him real good. He gasped and then got mad.

"You stinker!" he yelled. He picked up a clod of earth and threw it at me and then went dripping across the yard to find Mother. Will and I continued to carry water.

Clarkes' field and beyond was by this time mostly black. What had been yellow stubble bordered by aspen and birch decked in autumn colours was a charred battlefield with straw, floating ash and the tree trunks by now smoking snags. Down along the line fence where the land fell away too steeply for the binder to reach, an accumulation of dry stalks and weeds caught and went up with a great "swoosh," filling the air with black smoke and burning straw that drifted and settled in the yard and on the barn and house roofs. An old pile of slabs that had cascaded down the north creek bank from the sawmill, which had cut the lumber for the lean-to on our house, caught. They were tinder dry and bits of burning bark and sawdust climbed to the heavens in the vortex of smoke and flame, spreading and then settling, thousands of miniature glowing coals falling on everything. The heat down by the creek was intense. I had to shield my face with my arm as I hurriedly bailed up a bucket of water and beat a retreat. Father and my sister scrambled around cascading water down the shingles, snuffing small blazes and trying to keep as much wet as possible. The heat was drying it almost as fast as they poured water on. Will and I lugged bucket after bucket from the creek.

The horses were dancing around, pulling on their halter shanks and rattling the harness. I guess hot sparks were landing on them.

Amazingly, neither chicken house nor pigsty showed any sign of burning. They were further away and their roofs were made of poplar slabs—not as volatile a material as dry cedar shingles. They would probably have burned quickly if they had caught, but we were too busy attending to the house and barn to do anything about protecting them.

Mother came down the path with a couple of pots from the kitchen, filled them and made her way laboriously back up the hill, stopping every few steps to catch her breath. She was gasping and tears were running down her face. She was not paying any attention to the fire. I watched her as she went back to the house. I was afraid and sorry for her. Instead of passing the water up to my sister she carefully poured it on her geraniums, the one bright spot in the smoky ash-covered yard that she could cling to, something normal. The strain was becoming too much for her. She and this rough Alberta homestead had never come to terms. I doubted they ever would. The fire was just one more crisis that was defeating her.

Thankfully, on our side of the line fence there was nothing to burn. The stock had nibbled it down to almost bare earth as they loitered around the barnyard and the creek banks. This barrier and the creek were what was saving us. If we could just keep the roofs wet . . .

We hadn't eaten anything since breakfast and the creek water we were drinking wasn't very filling. It was well into the afternoon and we were all tired and hungry, our faces and clothing blackened with soot and our eyes red rimmed and smarting. Mother called and asked if we wanted to come in for tea, just as if it was another ordinary working day in which we could pause at any time. She couldn't bring herself to believe we were in any danger. I guess she didn't want to think about it. We just had to stay where we were, although it began to look like the worst was past. The front of the fire had burned its way east beyond the buildings leaving only smouldering logs and stumps. The slab pile was mostly gone, reduced to a pile of glowing ash in a matter of minutes.

"Billy!" Father called. "I've got to get down off this roof for awhile. My leg is bothering me. Can you come up?"

"Sure, Jack. I think we've pretty well got it beat, anyway. Come on down."

Father came down, negotiating the rickety ladder. When he reached the ground, his legs were shaking with the strain of balancing himself on the ridge for so long and maybe his leg, the one with the shrapnel scars on it, did hurt. So far today, though, he hadn't once mentioned his bad heart. I guess he realized that no one was going to give him much sympathy. He went into the yard by the house and he and mother stood close together, talking. She put her arms around him and they stood there for a few moments. I could tell she was crying. He turned and walked over to the team, leaving her standing there. His jaw was set and his face stern under its covering of black whiskers and soot. She wiped her eyes with her apron and went into the house.

Will sat on the barn roof, a bucket of water between his knees, watching the fire eat its way toward the road. His face was black, but he looked relaxed and he was whistling. I recognized the tune; it was one he often whistled. "Anitra's Dance," he'd said it was. He once told me that he used to play it on the piano. Mother had told us that she had played it too, but I had never heard her or Will play. Sometimes they talked, she and Will, about playing the piano.

I went into the house to see if I could find something to eat.

My brother was asleep on the kitchen couch and Mother was sitting beside him, her arm thrown protectively over him.

She didn't say anything; she just sat there looking straight ahead, her face streaked with soot, her grey hair dark with perspiration and her dress filthy.

"Do you want a sandwich?" my sister asked. She was cutting bread and slicing cold roast beef. Her dark hair was grey with ash, making her look old.

"Yeah I sure do, but aren't you supposed to be on the roof?" I asked.

"I've got it pretty wet. I'll go back up in a minute, but I got hungry."

"Make one for Will, too. I'll take it to him."

I took a couple of sandwiches and climbed up the ladder to the barn roof and sat on the ridge beside Will as we munched the sandwiches. From there I could see down to the road threading its way through the ravine. The front of the fire had advanced that far and was now consuming the log bridge over the creek. We wouldn't be going anywhere with the team and wagon in that direction.

All along the north side of the creek was a smoking ruin. Further away, smoke was still billowing as the fire chewed its way through thick bush toward the river. Clarke's homestead buildings were there. Maybe some of the neighbours had come to help him. The front would stop at the river. Without a strong wind, it wouldn't jump across. It would die there in the green wolf willow and horsetail reeds. It was almost there now.

From here on, our greatest danger lay further along the line fence between the buildings and the river, a distance of a quarter of a mile. The fire had jumped the creek and could work sideways, south into our grain fields in which stooks were still standing. It was burning close to the fence, setting some of the posts on fire.

Most of the danger to the buildings was past unless the wind changed, but even then the chance of coals hot enough to start a fire drifting back that far was minimal. Father, Will and I took some old sacks and buckets of water and started beating the flames that were nibbling their way into the field. We worked along, snuffing the whole south side right to the river. Once extinguished, we had a black fire break to protect us.

It was getting dark, the smoke hurrying the onset of night. The cows came wandering back, the discomfort of their full udders overcoming their reluctance to return to the smoky barnyard. My sister and I milked them as they stood in the field. They could stay there for the night. Father unhitched the horses. They had been standing there most of the day without food or water. He led them to the creek where they spent a long time drinking. He tied them to the fence and fed them. They would remain there until morning. There was still a danger to the barn if the wind got up in the night.

Suddenly I felt cold; the night chill was setting in. A dampness was dropping down and holding the smoke close to the ground. A long scarf of mist was forming over the river. What was left of the fire would die in the dampness.

There was still water to carry for the chickens and the sow, and we needed to wash; all of us were filthy. My arms and shoulders were aching; but with Will, whistling beside me, I made the final trips to the creek.

Lamplight was spilling from the window and smoke was rising from the stovepipe. A feeling of normalcy was returning. We washed most of the soot from our hands and faces and sat at the table in the kitchen. Mother seemed to have regained some of her composure and had found things for supper. We didn't care what it was, as long as it was food.

"I'll stay the night," said Will. "Somebody has to keep a watch. I'll bed down in the wagon box. I don't feel like walking back to my shack tonight. It may not be there, anyway, although I don't think the fire got that far south."

"There are quilts still in the wagon," Mother said. "They've got a few holes in them now from the sparks, but they will do for tonight. I'll have to mend them, though, before winter.

There are pillows too. But are you sure you wouldn't rather sleep here in the kitchen, on the couch?"

"No, I think I'll be better outside, just in case a wind does get up."

I went outside with Will. It was pitch black except where a myriad of firefly-like lights winked along our north side. Small flames, intent on consuming the last morsels of fuel before dying in the night dampness, still flickered. It would take many days and a good rain before the last coals would be extinguished. Deep down in the muskegs, the fire could burn all winter.

There was ash on the floors and furniture. It had seeped in everywhere. It cascaded off the bed when I threw the covers back to get in. Tomorrow would be a cleaning day like we had never seen before. There was the stink of burning, but the smoke was abating. I lay in bed beside my brother, twitching with tiredness and trying to work the cramps out of my legs. I wasn't worried tonight. I was sure we had cheated the fire. And besides, Will was out there in his wagon-box watch-tower, just in case there was a stray spark left. I could hear him through the open window, whistling the tune he mostly whistled: "Anitra's Dance."

7 • Will

THE TRUNK OCCUPIED SPACE IN OUR UPSTAIRS BEDROOM FOR almost five years. It crouched at the head of the stairs like a bulky misshapen beast, a thing to bump into in the dark. "A steamer trunk," Mother said it was, big enough to hold most everything anyone would need for an ocean voyage. A brutish old box with a domed top, it shed anything that was set on it.

The fabric covering, seen between its bruised and slivered oaken slats, was a scuffed tired green. On the corners the brass bindings had been wrenched away from the wood leaving sharp edges that seemed with deliberate malice to reach out to tear clothing, claw at bare legs, and lay careless fingers open. Frayed strings and bits of coloured paper attached to the handles were all that was left of the baggage tags that had over the years directed its fortunes, enabling it to find its way over the oceans of the world.

It was a well-travelled old trunk.

It was Will Sherret's trunk and it squatted there for two years without ever being opened. How he had come by it or when was never revealed, but it must have been well used even when he got it.

Will had come up the road one sunny Sunday morning in the spring of twenty-seven. He had a pack on his back with his coat draped over it and a double-bitted axe, the head wrapped in canvas, in his hand. We heard him whistling first. Then Judy, our border collie, her black and white ruff standing on end, went scooting under the fence to bark at him and sniff at his heels. Through the kitchen window we saw him unhook the big stock gate at the top of the hill and ease through into the farmyard. The horses snorted and shifted around. As he moved between them, their heads with ears perked forward, swung to face him. Whatever he said to Judy must have been reassuring; she quieted and wagged her tail and then trotted ahead of him, leading the way to the house.

Father got up from the breakfast table and went out on the porch, leaving the door open. He leaned against a post and watched him approach. Living on the fringes of civilization as we did, we didn't see many people. Someone coming to our door was an event.

"Finish your breakfast," Mother said. I was about to follow Father outside.

I jammed the last bite of toast into my mouth and chewed in a hurry.

"I'm done," I said and slid off my chair. I waited beside Father.

Will came through the garden gate, closed it behind him and walked up the path. He stopped at the step and looked up at us, a little smile playing with his mouth. His eyes, bright blue and friendly, peered out from a network of deep squint-wrinkles in a tanned face that supported a nose too large for it. He looked to be in his late thirties, a medium-sized man, built slim. His dress was that of the country: almost-new bib overalls, the bottoms turned up a couple of times and a faded shirt that was clean but in need of ironing: "bachelor's clothes," Mother called them. A grey felt hat, long used to his head, shaded his eyes and in back, greying hair curling at the ends escaped below the brim.

"Good morning," said Father.

"Good morning," he said. "This is the Jones' farm, isn't it, and you are Jack Jones?" He let the axe handle slide through his hand until the head rested on the ground. He placed both hands on the end and leaned on it, balancing the weight of his pack.

"That's right," Father nodded.

"They told me in Edmonton that this was your place. I'm Will Sherret." His voice was soft and his words carefully formed.

"Edmonton! Well now . . . I didn't think anybody in Edmonton knew about us away out here at the end of the road. We don't see too many people come walking this far. You've come a long way. What brings you all the way from Edmonton?"

"Land, mainly. I've filed on the quarter section next to you—to the west. I'm heading back in there to see what it looks like. If I stay and prove up on it, I guess we'll be neighbours."

"I've been wondering how long it would be before somebody filed on that quarter. You say your name is Sherret. You're English?"

"Yes. . . London. I'm beginning to think of myself as Canadian, though, I'll probably not go back."

"Well, It'll be nice to have an English neighbour for a change. The rest of the country is all bohunks: Hungarians, Ukrainians, Germans. I can't talk to any of them. Drop your pack and come in. Have you had breakfast?"

He let his pack—a bulging khaki canvas bag with leather straps—slide from his shoulders, leaned his axe against it and hung his hat on the handle.

"If you can call jackfish roasted on a stick, breakfast, yes, I've had breakfast. I camped by the river last night."

He ruffled my hair and smiled at me as he crossed the porch to the kitchen door.

"Mother, this is Mister Sherret. Will, I believe you said." He looked at Will. "He's filed on the quarter next to us. He's English, thank heaven . . . somebody we can talk to."

"How nice," said Mother. "Come in. I'll put the kettle back

on. We've just had breakfast, but I can make you a piece of toast . . . if you'd like. You're welcome, you know."

"I say. That's good of you, Mrs. Jones. I could stand a cup of tea, and a piece of toast would be nice. I'm not really that keen on fish for breakfast."

That's how Will Sherret arrived.

He stayed that day. He spent most of it sitting at the table talking through dinner and then through supper. That night he slept on the couch in the kitchen. He left the following morning after breakfast, heading west through our pasture to find his homestead.

"He's a nice man," Mother said. "He seems quite cultured. From an upper class family, I would think. He can talk on practically any subject."

"Any subject except one," Father said. "Did you notice? We still don't know where he came from or anything about him. He was pretty close-mouthed about that."

"You're right, you know. He talked about pretty general things, but nothing that said where he came from. That's rather odd, don't you think?"

"It is, but then, maybe it wasn't intentional, but we'll keep an eye on him."

He came back that evening, had supper and slept on the couch. The next day and the next were the same. After about a week, he said something about staying on . . .

"If it wouldn't be too much trouble . . . just until I get a house built. I can pay you whatever it's worth."

"Oh, don't worry about it. What's one more mouth. It's good to have someone to talk to." Mother and Will had found a lot of common ground to talk over.

A routine set in which we barely noticed. He would leave in the morning carrying a lunch and sometimes a borrowed saw or some other of the few tools we had and return in time for supper. Except, inexplicably, the routine would sometimes get broken.

The first time it happened, the Rawleigh man was there.

Stevens, his name was, from up in the Paddle Valley. His buggy came rattling into our yard late one afternoon, a few weeks after Will arrived. Stevens usually came late—just in time for supper. In addition to the things he peddled, he brought information: news of people we seldom saw. He was one of the few links we had with our far-flung neighbours. While he opened his cases and arranged them in a semicircle on the kitchen floor, he would inquire as to our health, the health of our animals and the prospects of our crops, depositing anything of significance in the back corners of his memory; things he could dispense further along his route.

His was a general store in miniature—bottles and packages containing everything from liniments and salves for man and beast to spices, extracts of lemon, almond and vanilla, to baking powder, cocoa, and custard—all nestled in their separate compartments and giving forth a wondrous blend of smells as the hinged boxes were swung open. Now and then there would be a sample of something new to give away and always a bag of jellybeans stuffed in a corner from which one or two would be doled out into shyly extended hands.

"Don't eat them now. You'll spoil your supper," Mother always said as though duty bound to do so.

He was a natural storyteller, and during supper he would recount the goings-on up and down the country: who had died, who had got married, had babies, whose horses had run away, and whose potatoes had frozen last winter. He would leave before dark in time to get back to Clarkes' where he would spend the night and eat breakfast.

It was close on supper time when we saw Will come out of the pasture at the top of the hill, shambling along in his loose-jointed walk. He stopped to look down at our buildings and yard, a habit he had gotten into. Normally he would continue on down, whistling as he came. Not today. I guess he saw the Rawleigh man's rig, the single brown horse tied to the fence. Something about it troubled him, and he turned tail and hurried back the way he had come. We didn't see him again until the following evening. Strange behaviour we thought, but we didn't think too much about it. He didn't explain, and Mother didn't inquire closely.

"We mustn't interfere, you know. It's his business."

He seemed hungrier than usual that evening.

"The Rawleigh man was here yesterday," Mother said casually, watching his reaction.

"Oh! That's whose rig was in the yard?" he said. He seemed relieved and smiled a little.

"Yes. He usually comes about this time of year."

Mother didn't say anything further, and Will didn't seem to want to pursue the subject.

The next time, Frank Towns was there.

Frank was an itinerant photographer who passed through now and then following the river, taking pictures—so he said—of the changing seasons. He habitually dressed like Johnny Canuck: in high laced leather boots, breeches and a stiff-brimmed scout hat. Seen at a distance, he could be mistaken for a policeman, but that had never occurred to us until the day Will first saw him. He and Father were talking in the yard when Will came to the top of the hill. He barely paused; he just whirled around and disappeared into the bush. We didn't see him for three days that time. In the course of conversation following his return, Father explained who Frank was.

"He looks like a policeman," said Will. Father agreed, but assured him he wasn't. Later on in the evening, Will mentioned two or three times how much Frank looked like a policeman.

A week or so later, Father said, "We're going to town tomorrow, Will. Do you want to come with us?"

"Ah . . . No. I think not, but thank you." He thought for a moment, hesitated, and then I guess he put it out of his mind. "No. I won't go."

"Can we bring you anything?"

"Yes, if you wouldn't mind." He made a small list on a

scrap of paper, reached in his pocket and extracted a thick sheaf of bills. He peeled off a couple and handed them to Father.

"Will that be enough?"

Father looked at the list.

"Yes, more than enough."

"I'll need the tarpaper soon. I'm almost ready to put the roof on. And I'm almost out of nails."

"I'll pick them up. It's no trouble." said Father.

"He's not broke anyway," I heard him remark to Mother, later on.

I watched Eddie pack our groceries into cardboard boxes while Father talked politics to the few loungers occupying the chairs by the stove. The general store was the meeting place, even in the summertime when the stove was just something to lean on. Jim Grant, the station agent, banged his way through the screen door. He handed Eddie a parcel and then turned to join the discussion.

"By the way, Jack," he said as Father made to leave. "Have you ever heard of anybody by the name of Sherret in these parts."

"Yes, matter of fact, I have. There's a man by that name putting up at our place. He's staying with us until he gets a shack built. He's filed on the quarter section west of us. Why?"

"There's a trunk sitting down at the station for a W. J. Sherret. Been there for a couple of weeks. Could it be the same guy? Came from somewhere in Manitoba. You want to take it to him?"

"It's probably him all right. Odd fellow, nice enough though. I could take it . . . might as well. It must be him."

We swung around by the station and picked up the trunk, loaded it in the wagon and hauled it home.

And that's how the trunk arrived.

Father and Will humped it up the narrow stairs to our loft bedroom; there was really nowhere else to put it.

"Just until I get my house finished," Will said.

My sister and brother and I stood around expecting him to open it right away, but he didn't. He went back downstairs.

"Your trunk was shipped from Manitoba. You were there at one time?" Father said, fishing around.

"Yes, at one time." He didn't offer anything more, so Father let the subject drop.

"I bet I know what's in that trunk," my brother said that night as we were talking in bed.

"What's in it?" my sister said. She reached out and pushed the end of the screen that separated her bed from ours to one side.

"I bet he's a magician and there's a lot of magic stuff in it."

"I bet there isn't. I bet it's full of money. I bet he's rich and he has all of his money in it."

During the next two years, it became a guessing game. When we couldn't think of anything else to talk about in the few minutes before sleep overtook us, we would guess what was in the trunk. It settled in as a fixture, there at the head of the stairs. It got kicked in passing; it got in the way and it collected dust, but it didn't get opened.

Will also settled in. He came and went without any set pattern. If Father indicated that an extra hand would be useful, he would pitch in and help with the farm work. He wasn't skilled as a farmhand, but he was willing.

He could talk by the hour, sitting over a cup of tea in the afternoon or after supper, but he seldom mentioned anything about his life in Canada. Little by little, though, he did let drop things about his boyhood and his young adulthood in England. Several times he spoke wistfully of his membership in the Junior Carleton Club, an exclusive London fraternity.

"He's an aristocrat; that much is evident," Mother said.

"He'll never make a farmer, and that much is evident too," said Father. "He's just not cut out to be a farmer. The farm spirit isn't there. I don't think he even likes farming. I think he's hiding from something. He avoids people. He never goes anywhere there might be people. There's something funny about him."

"Hiding! You don't suppose he's done something dreadful, do you?"

"I doubt he's done anything really bad, but I'm certain he's done something."

"Maybe he's a remittance man, some sort of a disgrace in the old country, you know."

"He might be, but no one sends him any money. He never gets any mail. On the other hand, he always has money in his pocket, quite a bit of money. A strange one, he is."

Will and I got along from that first day. He never became impatient with me when I followed him around. In fact, he encouraged me. We talked about a lot of things, sitting on the sawhorse at the wood pile or the bench at the end of the veranda.

"Has anybody ever told you about Bill the corn curer?" he said one day.

"Bill the what! Who was he?"

"I'm just kidding. His real name was William the Conqueror, and he was an English king."

"No. I don't know about him."

There began my first British history lesson. Will could talk on British history any time, and he was never boring. Whenever we had an opportunity, he would tell me about England's past. The way he spoke, he loved England, and I couldn't imagine why he had left it to come here to the Alberta bushland, but he always avoided questions along those lines. Most of the British history that came my way later on in school was old hat. I knew about it, and it was never as interesting.

Toward late summer he announced that his house was finished. He would no longer sleep on our couch or eat at our kitchen table. He gave Father a long list of groceries and several bills from the sheaf in his pocket.

"The next time you're in town . . . if you wouldn't mind . . . " he said.

"If you like, I'll still bake bread for you; an extra loaf now and then is no trouble." Mother said.

"Oh. Well—yes. That's very good of you. I'd like that."

Father gave him an old cast-iron box heater that had been sitting unused in our shed for a long time. He borrowed the team and wagon to freight it home. We half expected him to take his trunk, but he didn't.

"I'd like to take the boy back to my place, just for the day," he announced one morning a few weeks later. He'd helped to bring in the second cut of hay and stayed overnight. We'd played rummy, sitting around the kitchen table until it was too dark for walking home through the bush.

"Oh, wow! Gee, neat." It was an exciting offer. "Can I go, Mom?" I couldn't wait to see Will's house. With all his talk about royalty and nobility, I was sure it would be some kind of castle.

"Are you sure you want him for a whole day?"

"Yes, of course. I'd just like him to see where I live. I'll have him back before dark."

"Are you sure you want to walk that far?" she said to me.

"It's not far. Will walks it all the time." I grabbed my jacket. "I'm ready."

It was something more than a mile, across our place and part of Will's quarter. We talked—I guess I did most of it—as we walked, following the wheel tracks that wound between the sloughs and poplar trees in our pasture.

"How much farther is it?" I asked, expecting at any moment to see towers and battlements rising above the forest.

"It's not much further."

The trees thinned a bit and Will stopped. He was looking ahead and smiling. I couldn't see anything except leaves and white poplar trunks.

"There it is," he said.

"Where?" I couldn't see anything.

"Over there." He pointed and moved to one side. I still couldn't see anything. I kept walking. We were practically on

top of it before I saw it. It blended so perfectly with its surroundings, it could have risen from the ground itself, and it
was nothing like what I had expected.

It was small, little bigger than a chicken coop and because
it was so small, it looked higher than it really was. It leaned,
as well, as though being forced over by a strong wind. It was
made from small unpeeled poplar poles from which the bark
was beginning to shed in long ragged strips. He had plastered
in between them with mud that had greyed as it dried, giving
the whole thing an earthy look. The tarpaper-covered roof
was flat with a slight slope. A stove pipe stuck up through it
at an angle opposite to the lean of the walls. It had a rough-
lumber door, but no windows. The clearing where it stood was
small and stubbled with stumps from which the building
poles had been cut.

"Let's go inside," said Will enthusiastically. He had a boy-
ish pride in what he had to show me. He probably knew I
would approve, no matter what it was like.

It was gloomy and close inside. A little light leaked in
around the door and gaps in the chinking, but not enough
so to see anything we had to keep the door open. The floor
was native earth, just as it was created, except now it was
trampled and dusty. His sparse furnishings offered little in
the way of comfort. Along the back was his bed. It took up
most of the wall. It was a bunk made from poles over which
was spread a matting of slough grass and on that were a
couple of grey wool blankets. His only stove was our old box
heater. He'd made cupboards from stacked wooden apple
boxes and a table from split poles nailed against the wall.
Hanging from an overhead wire clothesline were his spare
overalls and in cloth sacks those of his groceries that could
be eaten by mice.

It had taken him a whole summer to get this far with his
homesteading.

"How do you like it?" he asked.

"Neat," I said. It really was neat. I couldn't imagine living in it, but it was neat because Will had made it. It was a far cry from what I had envisioned. A castle it wasn't.

He took a bucket, and I followed him down a narrow pathway, a hundred yards or so to a spring where he had excavated a shallow catch basin. This was his well. He filled the pail, scooping up the water with a pot.

"I'll build a fire and put the kettle on. Are you hungry?"

I wasn't very hungry, but I said yes anyway. He was trying hard to entertain me.

He built up a roaring fire in the old heater, filled a battered enamel kettle and set it on top. By the time it boiled, the inside of the cabin was stifling.

Lunch was eggs from our own grey speckled chickens, fried in lard and served on grey enamel plates, and bread carved from one of Mother's huge loaves. That was it. He served it with a flourish as though he was a waiter in a fine restaurant. We ate outside, sitting on logs. The eggs congealed on the cold metal plate faster than I could eat them. He poured tea into metal cups that matched the plates. The rim burned my lips as I sipped. It was strong and black, untamed by either sugar or milk. Later he brought out a paper bag of dried prunes for dessert.

I was sitting eating prunes and spitting the pits over a log, when he suddenly jumped up and went into the shack. He reappeared in a few minutes carrying a cloth-wrapped bundle. He laid it on top of a stump and unfolded it. Inside was a large pistol and a flat yellow box of cartridges. I had never seen a pistol, other than in pictures, and I couldn't take my eyes off it. It glinted wickedly in the sun, a sinister looking weapon of blued steel with a curving black, chequered grip.

"Have you ever seen a revolver?" Will asked.

"Gee, no. What kind is it?"

"It's a Smith and Wesson, thirty-eight calibre."

He opened it, took a handful of fat brass cartridges from the box, poked them into the chambers, and snapped it shut. I was nervous, not having been around guns very much.

Father had a rifle, but it was always out of reach, hung on nails high on the wall. Whenever he took it down to go hunting or to kill an animal we were butchering, we were always admonished to stand well back. And now, there was Will standing in front of me with a loaded pistol in his hand. I didn't know what to say.

He suddenly whirled, crouched, took aim at a woodpecker that had been hammering its way into a dry stump all the while we were eating and fired. It was a tremendous bang that made me jump and set my ears to ringing. The bird, startled but unscathed, swooped away with a "Yuk Yuk Yuk" to the back side of a dead poplar.

Will didn't comment. He ejected the spent shell and the remaining cartridges, placed them back in the box and began wiping the pistol with the cloth it had been wrapped in.

"How come you have a pistol, Will?" I asked.

"Some time I may need a pistol. Sometimes it's necessary to carry a firearm and you don't want people to see you doing it."

"Do you carry it around sometimes?"

"Not often, but sometimes."

Would I have a story to tell my brother and sister that night in bed. I could hardly wait.

Will's enthusiasm seemed to evaporate. I guess he had shown me everything that he thought might impress me. In fact, he looked a little shamefaced, as though he suddenly realized he had been showing off. He took the pistol, bundled in its cloth, into the shack and buried it in the hay on his bunk.

"Well, I guess it's time to go home," he said. There was still most of the day left.

We were quiet on the way home. Something had come between us, a kind of embarrassment.

After we had talked about pistols for a while that night in bed, my brother said, "I bet that trunk is just full of pistols . . . and maybe big knives."

I doubted it, but I wouldn't have been surprised if it didn't contain one or two other interesting things.

Mother and Father looked at each other with raised eyebrows when I told them about the events of the day and afterwards, I heard them talking in low tones.

Will didn't come down through the pasture and after a week, we began to be concerned.

"I wonder if he's sick," Mother said.

A few more days went by.

"I think I'll take a walk back there and see if he's all right," Father said. "Do you want to come along?"

I wanted to come along.

The door was closed and fastened with a piece of wire wrapped around a nail. Father undid it and pushed the door open. A stale smell—a mixture of wood, dead ashes, earth, sweaty clothes and fried food—met us. Will wasn't inside. His pack and his spare clothing were gone, and there were no groceries hanging from the line, but his blankets were there. On the table was a note on a scrap of paper held down with cup. "Have gone for a while," was all it said.

He came out of the pasture in mid-December. I saw him first. He was stopped, looking down into our yard. Then he continued down the hill, the powdery snow flying up around his rubber boots. He had on a worn mackinaw coat and a cap with earflaps, slightly small for his head and leaving his ears exposed. He was unshaven and his large nose was runny. His clothes had suffered, being more worn and faded than I had ever seen them. He wore an apologetic look as he came into the kitchen.

"Well. I see you're back," said Father, stating the obvious.

"You've been away," mother said, as though she'd just noticed.

"Yes," he said. "I went down east." He didn't expand.

He settled back into his routine, his visits becoming more frequent during the winter. I guess his shack was a pretty bleak and lonely place.

Come spring, Father had to go to hospital . . . something to do with the effects of the great war. He was gone for a month.

Will pitched in. He walked for hours behind our plough and our team, coaxing them along, the reins tied together and looped around his shoulders. He wasn't a good ploughman, but our fields were small and by the time Father returned, he had most of the land ready for planting.

He didn't seem to worry that his own place was still largely the way he had found it. He had no driving ambition to break any land. He just lived there in his shack when he wasn't at our place. He went away every once in awhile, never saying where he was going or for how long. He always had money for the things he wanted, and the sheaf of bills in his pocket never seemed to get any smaller. He didn't spend anything on clothing. His shirts and overalls became more raggedy. Mother patched them until there were patches on the patches, and she darned his socks. He didn't seem to care about his appearance.

He and Mother spent long hours talking about England, about books, the theatre, and about playing the piano. I couldn't imagine Will's dry, dirt-stained hands playing the piano, but if he said he could play one, then I believed him, even though I had no idea how a piano was played or what a one sounded like.

"I don't know how good a pianist he is, but he knows music," Mother said.

It was almost two years to the day. We were sitting at the table talking in the afternoon after Sunday dinner, when without commenting on what he was about to do, Will stood up, fished in his pocket for a small key, went upstairs and unlocked his trunk. My brother and sister and I scrambled up after him, as soon as we realized what he was up to. The mystery was about to unfold.

The lid crackled as it opened and a dry, musty smell escaped. The first thing that met my eyes was the paper lining inside the dome. On it was a scene: an ethereal landscape with pink cherubs and scantily clad women lounging in an open glade. I was fascinated by it.

Will began lifting things out. There were a few books, but mostly it was full of clothing: shirts, jackets, coats and several pairs of black glossy shoes. He unfolded each piece and spread them on our beds.

"Hmmm, moths!" he said. Mother heard him.

"Moths, did you say?" Mother was death on moths. She came upstairs.

"Oh dear! Oh dear! They certainly have been busy."

She lifted a black coat. It had long tails. The front was riddled with moth holes. Now that she was upstairs, she took charge. She insisted that Will take everything out to air it.

"None of this has been worn since I left England," he said. "There's little occasion to wear it out here."

"It's all pretty dressy. Is that a tuxedo? and my, my, full evening dress. You must have looked grand. Did you wear a top hat as well?"

"Yes. It's here somewhere." He rummaged around until he found it. He tapped it and it sprang open.

"I told you it was full of magic stuff," my brother said, wide-eyed.

Little had been spared. The moths had dined long and well. Will stood there looking at it. He stroked the shiny lapels on a jacket and rubbed the toe of a shoe on his sleeve. He looked sad and far away.

"I don't know whether anything can be mended," Mother said. "I could try."

"No. I wouldn't bother. It's no longer important."

He folded everything carefully and repacked it while we watched. Mother shook her head, "What a shame."

He lowered the lid and locked it. It sat there for another three years without ever being opened.

"I bet I know what's in that trunk," my brother said one night in an effort to get the old game going.

"We all know what's in it," said my sister. "Go to sleep."

There was no mystery left.

Father's absences at hospital became more frequent and prolonged. Mother struggled to cope with the farm work, but she had little aptitude. Little by little, worry, poverty and loneliness worked on her. She became vastly overweight and ill. Will kept things going as much as he could, but he too suffered from ineptitude, loneliness and—I suspect—homesickness for England. Whatever had brought him to the backwoods in the first place was also eating at him. He became more fearful of people. Even a minor thing out of place in our farmyard, something as simple as a gate left open, was enough to send him scurrying back to his shack. He still went away, but these excursions became shorter.

In 1931, the fire that nearly wiped us out went through. Will was a tower of strength during that crisis time.

In 1932 with both Mother's and Father's health failing, they talked long and hard about the future of farming and the prospects of children growing up without the benefit of schooling. The decision was never in doubt. We would sell out and leave the farm. We found a small place in town and moved in the fall. Will moved into the farm house to look after things until we could sell the animals and dispose of the land. I only saw him once after we moved.

The following spring I was sent from town with a message for him. I walked the five miles and arrived in the afternoon. He wasn't there. I wandered around the next-to-deserted place until dark, feeling sad and lonely. The house had a stale smell and was littered with the husks of flies. It was hard to recreate it as our home. I went upstairs where we had slept for so long. Will's trunk was still there, covered with dust. There was probably only dust inside by now. Outside, the animals and machinery were gone, sold at auction. Judy was gone. She had died on the horns of an old cow that had long since become beef.

There was nothing to eat in the cupboards, but a few hens still scratched in the farmyard, so I rummaged through the nest boxes in the chicken house for eggs. I hard-boiled and ate them, sitting on the old bench at the end of the veranda and then crawled into Will's bed. The screens on the doors and windows were rusted away and hundreds of mosquitoes sought me out. I slept very little. I lay listening to the river, a night sound that had soothed me since babyhood.

The following morning I saw Will at the top of the hill, looking down at the farm yard. I went outside and waved to him. I half expected him to turn and hurry away, but he recognized me, waved back and then continued on down.

We sat and talked for a long time about inconsequential things, but also about school and whether they taught British history. He was thin and haggard looking. His clothes were in tatters and not very clean. His eyes that used to be friendly had a hard glittery look.

As I was about to leave, he reached out, took my hand and shook it, the only time he had ever done that and the first adult to ever shake my hand.

"Goodbye," he said. " I probably won't see you again."

"Sure, Will. You could come and visit us in town,"

"I think not," he said.

It was a cold miserable day in November. Hard snowflakes were driving out of the north into my face as I walked home from school. For reasons I couldn't account for, I felt depressed. Mother would describe the feeling as "having the hump."

"We have some bad news," Father said as I came in the kitchen.

"What. What's happened?" I asked.

"Will is dead."

"Dead! How can that be. How do you know? He wasn't even sick."

"Roberts, the coroner, mentioned it. He had to investigate. He didn't die because he was sick. Roberts said it was suicide. Somebody found him in his shack."

"Suicide! No, not Will. He wouldn't commit suicide."

"Roberts is certain he did. He shot himself. There isn't much doubt . . . "

I couldn't imagine will doing that. Then I remembered a blue steel pistol lying on a stump in a sunny clearing. "Some time I may need a pistol." I heard Will say.

The letter came in 1939 although I wasn't there at the time. It came from Winnipeg and it found Father in Vancouver. It had been forwarded from back home in Alberta. I was no longer living at home, but Father told me about it. It was from a detective of some kind and it was directed to Father because for a few years prior to leaving Alberta, he had been a Justice of the Peace.

"We are seeking information about a William Sherret who is believed to have lived in your district in the late 1920s and early '30s. He may, in fact, still be there. If you know anything of his whereabouts, would you please advise.

We suggest you do not say anything about this letter to Mr. Sherret as there is some belief that he may be dangerous. In 1927, he is alleged to have absconded with the receipts of a farmers' co-operative organization in Brandon, Manitoba, and later, 1928 to 1934, he is suspected of being the person responsible for a series of robberies from business and banks in eastern Alberta, Saskatchewan and Manitoba. If he is still in the neighbourhood, please get in touch with us immediately."

"Hogwash! I can't believe that's Will," I said. "Did you reply? What did you tell them?"

"I told them that I had never heard of anyone by that name."

8 • Frank Towns

FRANK TOWNS LOOKED EXACTLY LIKE WHAT HE WAS: A MAN OF THE wilderness, all browns and greens blended together like the patterns in the forest. His face without trace of moustache or beard and his meaty arms below the rolled up sleeves of his green shirt were tanned the colour of old leather. His hair was brown. His khaki whipcord breeches—held in place with both belt and suspenders—disappeared into the tops of brown, high laced leather boots. The load on his back was brown and olive green. It was suspended from his shoulders by brown leather straps and to his brow with a broad leather tumpline. A brown, stiff-brimmed, Baden-Powell scout hat hung by a thong from his pack.

Father and I were in front of the barn in the spring sunshine when he arrived.

I was holding Prince's halter and talking to him, trying to reassure him that Father, who was trimming his hooves with a wood-chisel and hammer, wouldn't hurt him. Although as the sharp steel bit into the flared hoof, grown long during the winter, my own toes tended to cringe inside my boot. The big stock gate creaked, and Judy, a low growl welling in her throat, made a beeline for the mountain of a man easing his way through it. He paid no attention to her but closed the gate and came toward us. Judy stopped, nonplussed, and then skirted around behind him to steal a sniff at his boots. Father looked up from where he was kneeling.

"Good morning," he said. There was no reply. The big man stood looking at us from under his tumpline without saying anything. His load swayed as he shifted its weight and the straining leather straps creaked with each small movement.

Father pared a little more from Prince's hoof and stood up. "Are you lost or something, or are you looking for somebody?" he asked.

The man blew noisily through his nose, like a winded horse, and moved his mouth with a chewing motion, but no sound came out. He looked away, as if intent on examining the new barley showing green in the south field, and then back again, his face twisted as though in pain.

"Towns . . . " The single word trailed off, and he quickly averted his eyes.

"Town!" said Father. "If you're looking for town, you've come a long way in the wrong direction."

"Towns. Frank Towns . . . I ah . . . "

"Oh! Your name is Frank Towns. Is that it?"

"Yes." He looked embarrassed as though blurting out his name was the wrong thing to do. His face got a deeper brown and he half turned away, swinging his pack around.

"I'm Jack Jones." Father said. "This is my place. Are you looking for me?"

"No . . . ah . . . yes, I think." he said, half turning back again. "The river . . . "

"The river? It's over there." Father gestured toward the line of willows at the edge of the field.

He turned completely away until he was looking directly at the log wall of the chicken house.

"I'm Frank Towns. I'm a photogra-a-apher, and I wa-ant to take pictures . . . along the river, there." This information tumbled from his lips and came to us over his shoulder, a strange mixture of drawl and oddly-formed words.

"Oh! I see," said Father, sidling around to get in front of him. He kept turning away.

"I want to ca-amp . . . here, somewhaere, for a few days. Is tha-at a-all raght?"

"Yeah, sure. I guess so, but if you're not in a hurry, why don't you drop your pack and come in and have a cup of tea and a bite to eat, and we'll talk about it? We don't see very many people down here. You say your name is Towns, eh? Can't say I've ever heard of you."

"What about Prince?" I asked.

"You can let him go," Father said. I unsnapped the rope from his halter and whacked him over the rump with it. He arched his neck and trotted off toward the creek, seeming pleased with his tidied up toenails. Frank turned to watch him go. A little smile softened the worried look on his face.

"Come on to the house," Father said. "Get that load off your back. It looks pretty heavy."

He didn't reply. He just nodded and followed Father to the garden gate. I came behind, looking at what he was carrying on his back.

It was a substantial load. He walked bent forward to balance it. Its base was a bulging canvas packsack, stained and worn, attached by the leather straps to his shoulders. On top of it, tied to the straps, was a roll of canvas with brass grommets that looked like it could be a tent. On top of that was a bundle of grey wool blankets, wrapped around some odd-shaped object and tied with stout cord. Capping it off was a squarish parcel around which canvas was carefully folded and tied with rope in a sort of diamond hitch that criss-crossed the entire load, holding it all together. The top extended above his head. The whole effect was that of a moving mountain, and it dwarfed Father's short stocky figure.

As I followed the big man's wake, I could smell his sweat mixed with the scent of spruce and smoky camp fires, a smell like newly-made Indian moccasins that appeared on the shelves of Keely's hardware store in the fall. He strode beside Father to the veranda where he lifted the tumpline from his brow and let the straps slide from his shoulders. The muscles in his arms bulged as they caught the weight and lowered it to the ground. He took a blue bandanna from his hip pocket and wiped his brow.

My brother Owen, five years old and curious, came off the veranda and stood looking at the pack against the wall. He squatted beside it, reached out and ran his hand over the smooth leather straps and fingered the buckles, a look of delight and wonder on his face.

"Come inside," Father said.

Frank ducked as he went through the door. Father and Mother were short people and the door had been made to accommodate them—with little to spare.

"Can you put the kettle on, Mother?" Father said. "This is Frank Towns, a photographer. He says he's come to take pictures of the river." He turned to Frank.

"This is my wife and my daughter."

Frank took one look at Mother, glanced quickly at Olwyn and then swivelled around to face the door. His mouth worked without a sound coming out of it and his face contorted.

"Good morning, Mr. Towns," said Mother. "Have you come far? . . . and carrying that big pack, too. My, it must be heavy." She filled the kettle and put it on the stove, removed a lid and gave the fire a prod with the lifter.

Frank stood, filling the small room with his bulk and his smoky odour, his hands hanging slack, shifting from one foot to the other. His brown hair brushed the underside of the ceiling beams. He looked first at the floor, then at the wall, and then out the door, but made no effort to speak. He just nodded. Father looked at Mother and shrugged.

"Sit down, why don't you?" Mother said. "I'm making tea. It will be ready in a few minutes."

He reached around, grasped the back of a chair, pulled it away from the table and sat down facing the door. The chair suddenly looked fragile and spindly under his huge frame and it creaked as his weight came on it. My sister looked at me and grinned. I knew she half expected it to collapse. The rungs were loose in all our chairs, and occasionally one did. Father seated himself across the table and addressed Frank's broad back.

"Tell me, now. You were saying you want to camp. And you said you take pictures. What kind of pictures do you take and what do you do with them?" Father didn't usually ask a lot of questions of a stranger, but Frank wasn't volunteering much.

"The govvm . . . the govvvment buys them." If he didn't look directly at anyone, it seemed that his speech came a little easier although his words fell all over each other in getting out. He sounded like he had forgotten how to talk, and perhaps he had. From what he told us in hesitant bursts he was a loner, spending months on end by himself, ranging the wooded benchland along the river and taking pictures for Government publications.

He thawed gradually, becoming more at ease with successive cups of tea. And he gradually shifted around so that he was only half facing away. However when he spoke, he still turned his head to either look at the ceiling or out the window. Mother, always one to take full advantage of a visitor, plied him with questions and with lunch, and she chatted away most of the afternoon, sitting at the table or puttering around in the kitchen. Frank was more of a person to talk to than to talk with, and Mother needed a change, someone who wasn't Father or us to direct her thoughts to, even if there was little response.

"You'll stay for supper—won't you?" she said at about four o'clock.

"Ah . . . yes. Thaat would be fine . . . missus . . . "

The novelty of a stranger and the adult conversation soon wore thin for Owen and me and after an hour or so, we went back outside. Owen was still fascinated by the straps and shiny buckles on the pack leaning against the porch. He kept fingering and rubbing them. There was something going on in his mind.

He could eat, Frank could; his massive frame must have needed a lot of groceries to fuel it. He tucked into the roast beef and potatoes. It was plain fare, but probably better than he ate on a lot of days. He lived off the land, he'd said. Since he didn't carry any kind of a gun, his diet would have to consist mostly of fish, snared rabbits and whatever wild berries were in season. He sat sideways to the table with his plate in his lap, not looking at us if he could help it. If Mother or Father said anything requiring an answer, he addressed his replies to the window or the ceiling.

It was light in the evening, long after supper was over. Frank came out and shouldered his way into his pack straps. He had refused an invitation to spend the night on the kitchen couch.

"You can camp over there in that little thicket if you like," Father said, "to the left of that snag there, on the edge of the gully."

He looked where Father was pointing in the direction of the snag and nodded.

Mother came out on the porch. "Come and have supper with us tomorrow night," she said. "You might as well eat with us while you're here."

He ducked his head in a nod. "Thaanks . . . missus."

"We'll show you where to go," I said. Owen and I ran ahead of him along the path that skirted the edge of the barley.

He began by limbing off a couple of poplars with a hand axe and clearing the ground between them. To these he fastened the ridge rope of his tent, pulling it fiddle-string tight, his great arms and shoulders bulging as he rccfed on it. He pegged it down with stakes at the four corners. There was no floor in it. He denuded a young spruce of its branches and heaved them inside, arranging them loosely into some semblance of a bed. Over this he spread a piece of canvas. His home was complete. He had probably gone through the same motions countless times and the whole operation took him

127

only a few minutes. We watched. We would have helped, but he ignored us. It was as if he was completely alone.

He set the rest of his pack inside, picked up his hand axe and strode off down the gully to the river without a backward glance at Owen and me. We went home along the edge of the barley. The darkness dropped down, soft and woolly, relieved only by a handful of fat stars overhead.

"Bedtime," Mother said.

The window in our room above the kitchen faced the river. Through the screen came the liquid sound of the rapids, a sound that was always there and so normal we were seldom conscious of it. Owen and I stood on our bed, leaning on the log windowsill and looking out at the darker bulks of the barns and outbuildings across the yard.

"I hear something," Owen said.

"What do you hear. What does it sound like?"

"It sounds like music."

"Music!"

"Yeah—music. You listen."

"You're crazy."

"You listen. I can hear music. Listen to it."

I pressed my ear against the screen. The sound of the river, rising and falling in the darkness, was all that I could hear.

"I don't hear anything." I said.

"Listen! I can hear it."

We stood motionless straining our ears and trying not to make the bed squeak. Then I heard it, faint as it was and buried in the sound of the river.

"Yeah, I can hear it," I said.

"What are you listening for?" Olwyn asked, getting out of bed and coming to the window.

"Music," we said, "can you hear it?"

We crowded together, listening. We could all hear it. It rose and fell, varying with the sound of the river. Then it stopped. Strain as we could, it was no more.

"Where do you think it came from?" We asked each other as we crawled into bed.

The tent was still there in the morning, hardly visible from the house. It blended perfectly with its surroundings. Owen and I went for a look.

"Don't touch anything," Mother admonished us. "It's all right to look, but don't touch."

There wasn't much to see; the front flaps were closed and there was little else to look at. There was no sign of Frank.

He showed up at supper time, striding around the field.

"Ask about the music," I whispered to Mother.

She had been sceptical when we told her about hearing music in the night, but we all insisted that we had heard it, and the fact that it was music piqued her interest.

"These kids insist they heard music last night," she said to Frank. "Did you hear anything?"

"I played the gra-a-amaphone," he said, looking as though he had been caught at something not very nice. He reddened and turned away.

"Gramophone! did you say. You have a gramophone?" Mother looked incredulous.

"Yes."

"With records. You have a gramophone with records?"

"Two records. That's a-a-all."

"Well . . . my, my, a gramophone. Think of that. You carry it in your pack?"

"Yes."

"A gramophone in a packsack. I've never heard of it. What records do you have?"

"The 'Blue Damn Blue' and the 'Damn Blue Waves.'" He said, looking at the floor.

"The what?" said Mother.

"Stra-a-uss. You know. The 'Blue Damn Blue.' You know."

"Oh! Yes, of course. The 'Blue Danube Waltz.' And the 'Danube Waves,' of course."

"Yes."

"Maybe we could hear the gramophone play," I prodded Mother and whispered. "Could you ask him."

"I haven't heard the 'Blue Danube' for years," Mother said, "perhaps you could play it for us sometime."

"Yes, Missus," was all he said.

He doesn't want to, I thought, but I didn't want to prod Mother any more. She would just tell me to be quiet and later explain that it was his business if he didn't want to play his gramophone.

The following morning, Owen got hold of a gunny sack, filled it with tin cans, fashioned a tumpline out of binder twine and carried it all over the place. After an hour or so, the twine had cut into his brow and made a deep red mark. Mother finally took it away from him and despite his objections made him quit playing Frank Towns—as he called it—for awhile.

When Frank showed up at supper time, he was carrying the gramophone. The base, a wooden box on which the mechanism was mounted, was under his arm—it was the canvas-covered parcel that rode the top of his pack. A morning-glory shaped horn was in his hand; it was the odd-shaped thing that had been wrapped in his blankets. He assembled the two pieces and set it as a unit on the end of the table. All through supper, we looked at it. It had a faint oily smell and on the side was a picture of a small white dog gazing into a horn like the one on top.

"Before there's any gramophone playing, the dishes have to be washed and the chores done," Mother said.

The routine tasks—wood box filling, water carrying, chicken feeding and dishes—had never been done with less dawdling and complaining.

Mother took off her apron, the signal that the concert could begin. The kitchen chairs were arranged in a semicircle facing the table. The gramophone was moved to the middle.

Frank had the records, two cylinders about four inches long and two inches in diameter, wrapped in a piece of chamois tied with a shoe lace. He unwrapped them, his hands shaking with nervousness and his face red with embarrassment.

"Which one fiiirst?" he asked, not looking at us.

Mother looked at Father and he looked at her.

"Go ahead," he said, "you choose."

"Oh . . . I don't know—perhaps the 'Blue Danube.'"

Frank slid the cylinder onto the drum and then cranked the handle. He seemed to crank for a long time. He released the catch, and the drum began to turn. He lowered the needle onto it. There was a loud metallic hissing and scratching and then music. We knew the tune. Mother hummed it every so often, and once she had even tried to teach Olwyn and me to waltz to it. It was much faster coming out of the horn than she had hummed, but it slowed as the spring unwound. The 'Danube Waves' followed. I didn't know it, but it didn't matter.

Frank dutifully played both records several times, but the 'Blue Danube' got the nod as being the most popular.

"Well! thank you, Frank," Mother said, as darkness settled in and the kitchen became gloomy. He nodded, carefully wrapped the cylinders in the chamois and detached the horn from the mechanism.

I went to bed with the 'Blue Danube' ringing in my head.

In the morning, the tent was gone. All that was left was the pile of spruce branches between the poplars.

"An odd kind of duck," Father said. "Not too many around like him. He might, at least, have said goodbye."

"It was nice to have someone around for awhile, though. I wonder if we'll ever scc him again." said Mother.

We did see him again. One morning in the fall, the tent was there, looking exactly as it had in the spring as if it had never been away. Frank strode across the barley stubble at supper time. Mother had prepared extra; she knew he would probably be along. They talked—at least Mother did—sitting at the table.

"Ask him about his gramophone," I prodded Mother.

Yes, he still had it, but he didn't offer to play it again.

He came twice a year after that until we left the farm. He still carried a huge pack and the same kind of wrapped bundles rode on it, but we never again heard the gramophone play, not even carried along with the river sound rising from the rapids in the darkness.

Where he spent his days, he never said—perhaps taking pictures?

We never saw sign of a picture—or a camera for that matter. He never spoke much about taking pictures after that first day. In fact, he never talked much about anything. He was talked to, mostly. We wondered sometimes what he really did, alone out there, wandering the benchland.

In 1941, I was riding a Number 3 streetcar west on Hastings Street in Vancouver. I looked idly out of the window, and there was Frank, striding along. I would have known him anywhere; he was dressed the same. I got off at the end of the block, but he had disappeared, vanished, and I didn't find him.

I got back on the next streetcar. The 'Blue Damn Blue' came to mind. It still does, sometimes.

9 • The Late Starters

THE HALLWAY WAS A SHADOWY CAVE POPULATED BY THE INDISTINCT figures of children who all of a sudden became still and quiet as we entered. The only light came slanting in from two open doors that led to classrooms—one on either side—and was absorbed by the dullness of the grimy oiled floor, the brown wainscotted walls, and the drab overall- and windbreaker-clad throng waiting for the bell to ring. Its far end disappeared into gloom.

We followed Mother—confident that she knew where to go—a clutch of three half-grown chicks trailing a purposeful hen. Eyes, dozens of them, stared and stayed on us as we threaded our way through the crowd through a cloakroom and then into the classroom that opened beyond. The floor squeaked. It too was a dirty oiled brown. The walls, like those of the hallway, were wainscoted—the ones that weren't covered with blackboard. There were windows in the west wall, small panes that, although dirt encrusted, admitted enough filtered grey November light to illuminate the lacklustre furnishings: rows of worn desks, a teacher's desk facing them and, to the right of it in the corner, a brown cupboard that extended the height of the blackboard. The room was cold and smelled of floor oil, stale clothing, rubber boots and the hot dust of furnace pipes.

A woman sat at the desk staring out the window, her head propped on her hand, seemingly unaware of the foursome bearing down on her. We filed between the rows and arranged ourselves in front of her desk.

"Good morning. I'm Mrs. Jones," Mother said in a forthright tone. Mother was not intimidated by her surroundings; she had, after all, taught school for a lot of years in England and was quite at home in a classroom. The woman didn't stir; she continued to stare out the window. "I'm Mrs. Jones," Mother said again, raising her voice a notch, "and these are my children." The woman gave a start and looked around.

"Oh yes. Yes. Good morning."

Mother pushed us forward, one at a time, and introduced us.

"You are . . . ?"

"Ah . . . I am Miss Gaudreau. I teach here."

"Oh yes. Mr. Milhausen told me . . ."

She gave us a fleeting glance without acknowledging the introductions, stood up and moved from behind the desk. She didn't say anything more; she just looked at Mother, curious, I suppose, as to why we were intruding into her world first thing in the morning.

She being the teacher, I had already accorded her goddess-like qualities and, I guess I expected a goddess-like appearance, but instead my impression was that she was kind of homely. She was a tall young woman, much taller than mother who was barely more than five feet. Her hair was dark—not black as the raven's wing or anything that fanciful—just ordinary brown, but dark nonetheless and drawn back in an untidy bun. She had a large mouth and sleepy eyes that seemed to have trouble focusing. Her dark red suit was smudged in front with chalk dust.

"We have just moved here, to town that is, and I want to start the children in school," said Mother. "I spoke to Mr. Milhausen last week. He said they could start today."

"They should have started in September," Miss Gaudreau said accusingly.

"We weren't here in September. We have just moved."

"Oh yes. Of course. You said that, didn't you?" She smiled then, and an amazing array of white teeth erupted from between her lips and extended outwards to hang like a snowy cornice over the receding escarpment of her chin. "Where have they been going to school?"

"They haven't been going to school. We have been living on a farm where there was no school to go to."

She stopped smiling at that. "I'm afraid we can't take them then; there's no room in grade one." She said it with finality and then half turned away as if signifying that the conversation was at an end and, that being so, she expected us to leave.

"Oh. I'm sure they are all more advanced than grade one," said Mother. "They can all read and write and can do arithmetic. I have been teaching them at home, you know. I was a teacher at one time."

A look of consternation crossed Miss Gaudreau's face and then she bristled a bit. It seemed that this was not something she wanted to hear or deal with: us starting late in the school term and knowing how to read, write and do arithmetic—despite never having gone to school—and mother proclaiming that she was a teacher. She teetered on the edge of indecision, pondered for a moment and then said, "Well. There are two desks in the grade two row . . . the boys could go in grade two I suppose. The girl will have to go in grade three though; that's the only desk left."

"Does it matter where they sit?" It was Mother's turn to look perplexed.

"Oh yes. You see the desks are arranged in five rows. The grade one pupils are next to the blackboard, the grade twos are next and so on. The grade fives are next to the window. We can't mix them up. It would be too difficult . . ." Her toothy smile appeared again, as if the logic of what she had just said explained everything to everyone's satisfaction.

Mother's look of puzzlement deepened. What she had heard did not make a whole lot of sense, and she stood there studying Miss Gaudreau and trying to figure out if she had missed something.

From somewhere, the school bell rang and there was a sudden surging sound as that of a moving herd.

"Well. All right . . . I guess . . . If you are sure that's the way it has to be . . . but I think you'll find . . . Mr. Milhausen said . . . " She turned to go, unwilling, at this stage, to argue for a better deal. She looked at each of us in turn. "Now, do as Miss Gaudreau says. Be good, children." She hesitated, looked once more at Miss Gaudreau, who was still smiling and then made her way toward the door, buffeted en route, by the entering runny-nosed horde of those who would be our classmates.

We weren't sure which desks were to be ours, so we waited. We looked at Miss Gaudreau, expecting she would indicate our places, but she was behaving as if we weren't there. She had retreated behind her desk and was again looking out the window, her face blank. There was a lot of pushing and shoving— some of it for our benefit, I was sure—and staring at us, but after a few minutes of chaos, the desks were filled except for three. We hesitated and then sat in them. We were all at the back of the room.

I was eleven years old, my sister thirteen and my brother nine.

This was not the beginning but a furtherance of our education that had begun as soon as we were able to understand the spoken word. Mother had read to us from infancy from tattered books she had brought with her from England, and when they wore out she ad-libbed, entertaining us with stories of her own creating. She taught us to read. I must have been very young because I don't actually remember learning. I don't ever remember a time when I couldn't read. She taught us arithmetic as well, right up to long division and beyond.

We had little to read from. Much of what we read were books that were sent as gifts for Christmas or birthdays from relatives in England. They were all English stories and bore little relationship to the real world of an Alberta homestead. We read them anyway and then reread every last word until the books fell apart. Those, the occasional newspaper and the magazines we subscribed to were what we read.

I was six when the Department of Education offered correspondence courses to the far-flung families of the Alberta hinterland. Mother applied, and a parcel of school material came from Edmonton that September: grey paperback books, lesson plans and a list of exercise books and pencils to be purchased locally. We sat at the kitchen table that winter—and succeeding winters—and worked through the assignments.

Instead of immediately buying the specified number of exercise books, Father bought one, took it apart and divided it in three. And instead of three pencils, he again bought one and carefully divided it in three, being very exact, measuring and then sawing with his pocket knife. The piece with eraser went to my sister to avoid any suspicion of favouritism between my brother and me. The exercise-book paper was used for those assignments to be sent to the Department for correction. The daily practice assignments were done on brown wrapping paper, the kind with lines on it. As time went on, we did each get our own exercise books, and then there was the red letter day when we each got a new pencil of our very own.

Mother imposed classroom rules on us: sitting straight in our chairs, no talking, putting up our hands to request something and addressing her as Mrs. Jones, instead of Mom.

"You might as well get used to behaving yourselves and not talking," she said. "When, if ever, you do start school, you'll know how to conduct yourselves."

It was exciting to go to school. I had looked forward to it for most of a year, ever since we had decided to move to town. Mother had instilled into us the wonders of the world of books and learning. Father, on the other hand, did not ascribe as much importance to an education as she did. His had been little more than basic, and as far as he was concerned, that was all farm kids needed.

"I didn't get much education, and I've done all right for myself," he'd said more than once. Whether he was seeking approval for what he had accomplished without education or whether he was assuaging the guilt he may have felt at not being able to send us to school, I wasn't sure.

I expected teaching and learning to begin immediately. A door would open and there would be a vast storehouse of knowledge for me to pick and choose from. Little happened, though. Miss Gaudreau continued to look out the window, paying scant attention to the talking, jostling, stamping of feet and the squeaking of desks. When the noise finally reached a crescendo, she turned and with resignation rapped on the desk with her pointer and told everybody to stand and recite the Lord's Prayer. The droning and mumbling took but a minute after which there was more crashing and squeaking of reseating.

Everybody else knew what to do, and established routine took over. My sister and brother and I didn't know what to do. We hadn't brought any school books—we had understood that everything would be supplied by the school, but it wasn't—so we sat there at a loss. We weren't about to risk asking anybody around us where to get anything either. Not talking in school had been drummed into us by Mother. The fact that everybody else was talking didn't alter that. All the grade twos had textbooks of one kind or another and they dragged them out and began reading—or at least looking at them. Owen and I sat with our hands in our laps, feeling uncomfortable. Olwyn, across the aisle, was in the same boat.

With nothing else to do, I looked around the classroom. At the front above the blackboard and Miss Gaudreau's desk, a Union Jack was pinned to the wall and beside it, a portrait of King George V. Down one side of the blackboard, next to the grade one desks, was a column of words written in yellow chalk and partially smudged from long usage: cat, hat, rat and the like. Nothing else livened the high-ceilinged echoing room. There were no pictures, decorations or anything else to relieve the plainness.

My desk was a tight fit. At eleven, I should have been in the row next to the window or close to it. The desk's hardwood surface, the varnish worn thin by the scrubbing of sleeves, bore the marks of some former occupant who was handy with a jack-knife; his initials were incised deeply into the top, and a row of notches decorated the front edge. The inkwell in the upper right corner was stuffed with the husks of dead flies. It appeared that whoever he was, he'd had time to kill. There was nothing on the shelf underneath.

Our classmates—of whom I knew but one, Pauline Teer—ranged in size from tiny to huge. One kid, Everet, in the grade three row—he must have been thirteen or fourteen—was a monster. He was decked out in cowboy gear complete with studded belt and leather cuffs. He was shoe-horned into the desk that was never designed to accommodate anyone of his proportions. He kept turning to look at my sister and treating her to a vacant grin.

Miss Gaudreau, meanwhile, had roused herself and was writing assignments on the blackboard. Directly in front of the grade two row, she set out columns of arithmetic exercises: addition and subtraction, twenty problems in all.

"Grade two. Take out your arithmetic books and do these exercises," she said.

I put up my hand. "My brother and I don't have any exercise books. We don't have anything else either," I said when Miss Gaudreau looked at me. A snicker rippled across the room. I felt embarrassed.

"Will someone lend these children some paper and pencils?" she asked. We were proving troublesome that was plain in her voice and manner. The kid in front of me turned halfway round.

"You're not getting none of mine," he said.

Everybody seemed to be looking at us again, but nobody

offered to help. Pauline came to our rescue. She had a new exercise book. She took it apart and shared it between us. Miss Gaudreau found three stubs of pencil. We were back where we had started.

It was pretty simple stuff. I worked out the little sums and differences in a few minutes and then found myself listening to what was going on over in grade five country. When it came time for marking, we were told to pass our papers to the one behind, while Miss Gaudreau wrote the answers on the board. Owen was behind me so I passed my paper to him. There was nobody behind him, so he just kept his and marked it himself. I didn't give the kid in front of me the benefit of the doubt on anything. I marked most of his stuff wrong. That was it. There was no checking to see who had got what right.

At recess, we were the centre of attention. We were the freaks, the big kids in grade two. Could we play marbles, could we skate, play baseball and on and on. Because we had lived in isolation, we had grown up with English accents acquired from our parents. This was seized upon as something to make fun of. Olwyn was getting the same kind of hazing from the girls. It was cold out, so we stayed inside and hung around the cloakroom and hallway. There was a single big furnace register at the back of the room over which the girls congregated to let the heat blow up under their skirts.

The classroom on the other side of the hall was the high-school: grades six to eleven, presided over by Mr. Milhausen, a short wide man with a perpetual look of distaste pulling down on the corners of his mouth. His reputation was well-established and rock hard. Nobody fooled with Mr. Milhausen. Some time early in the term he had shaken a couple of kids so hard the buttons had popped off their pants. Since then, things had been pretty orderly in Mr. Milhausen's room.

The grade ones got to read the words on the blackboard right after recess. Miss Gaudreau went down the list with her pointer and each student read them off. The simple words were pretty liberally translated by most of the kids. Miss

Gaudreau did not pause to correct anybody; she just hurried down the list regardless of whether they read them correctly or not, a look of utter boredom written all over her. Apart from a few isolated periods of attention during the day, the grade ones spent their time with crayons and paper.

The grade twos got to read next. We gathered in a semi-circle around Miss Gaudreau's desk with grade-two reading texts in hand. Since Owen and I didn't have any, we had to borrow from the kids next to us. The story was an unsophisticated little yarn about a girl named Iris. Cecil, the skinny kid in front of me, read his paragraph, calling the girl Irma. Miss Gaudreau didn't correct him, nor did she correct any of the stumbling and mispronunciation by any of the others. She sat at her desk with the text open in front of her, but her mind was elsewhere.

It became apparent that getting through the day was the task Miss Gaudreau had set for herself—nothing more.

By the end of the day I had spent less than an hour doing assignments. The rest of the time I had listened to what was going on around me and waited for something meaningful to happen. Miss Gaudreau had extended herself to the point of preparing a list of school supplies and had given it to Olwyn to take home. It was a small list, but one that made a significant dent in Mother's budget. What made it harder to accept was that we had done the same lessons by correspondence. We were, however, no longer dependent on borrowed books and paper.

The boredom of that first day was followed on successive days by more of the same. We read the story of Iris, over and over, with Cecil calling her Irma and Miss Gaudreau not noticing. Miss Gaudreau may at one time have been an enthusiastic teacher, but it was evident that some kind of career dry-rot had set in and her enthusiasm had given way to indifference. I was thirsting for new things to learn. Most of the time there was nothing to do, but Miss Gaudreau made no effort to assign extra work; she just let me sit there.

There was the challenge of interacting with classmates—another facet of school I had looked forward to—at recess, noon hour and after school, but much of that was not pleasant. Owen and I were tested almost every day. Me more than Owen. He was a natural people-person who could turn aside conflict with a smile and a joke. I—more competitive by nature—found myself embroiled in wars of one kind or another much of the time. I gravitated to the older boys, but because I was only in grade two, I suffered ridicule. School was rapidly becoming a bitter experience, and I withdrew into myself.

My discovery of the library was the single most important thing that happened to me that year. It was in the corner cupboard where I had never seen anyone go but Miss Gaudreau. I had come back early from lunch, and there was no one in the room but Miss Gaudreau. The cupboard door was open so I looked in it. It was full of books.

"I doubt there are any books in there that would be of interest to a grade two," said Miss Gaudreau, coming up behind me. "You may look if you wish, though."

I wanted to say that I should be at least in grade four, but I didn't.

They were mostly thick hardcover books. The titles meant nothing to me. I took one anyway, choosing it because it was the biggest book there. It was Ernest Thompson Seton's *Wild Animals I Have Known*.

"May I read this one?" I asked.

"Its pretty old for a grade two, but yes. You may."

There was time to read, and I devoured that book. I read about Lobo, the King of the Currumpaw, Redruff, the Partridge, The Pacing Mustang and the Springfield Fox. I lived in that book for weeks.

After that there was *Wild Horse Mesa* by Zane Grey. I no longer cared what went on around me; I chased wild horses across the western plains. And later yet, I discovered a slim blue paperback book of Greek mythology. I sailed with Jason's

Argo, in quest of the Golden Fleece. I soared with Bellerophon astride his winged steed, Pegasus, and I assisted Perseus to kill Medusa. School took on a new meaning.

The dark days of winter dragged nevertheless. Christmas came and with it a school concert. I was petrified. There was no inducement that could make me go on the stage in front of our parents and the rest of the townsfolk. I dug in my heels. I guess I had a deep-rooted aversion to being noticed. Father's attitude was mainly to blame. He could forgive a lot of things, but being conspicuous was not one of them. He had instilled into us that to stand out was to attract attention and therefore notoriety. If we were being noticed, it followed that we were doing something wrong. His credo: children should remain in the background and behave themselves.

I had grown up acquiring a living fear of an audience.

The upshot was that instead of just being put down or ignored by Miss Gaudreau, I incurred her wrath. No matter. I wasn't going in her concert.

A side issue of the concert was to cause me to be noticed and assign me a measure of notoriety. It also put me deeper into the glue with Miss Gaudreau. There was a frog-faced kid in grade four who had dedicated his waking hours to making my life miserable. During one of the rehearsals he met with an accident that at the time, I was alleged to have caused. The girls were doing a drill with Indian clubs: those bowling-pin shaped weapons that were swung in various patterns, always by girls and ostensibly as an exercise. It was an activity that was popular at the time and one that the drill team would demonstrate at the concert. The desks were pushed to one side and the bigger girls were lined up in drill formation, swinging away. Frog-face and I got into a shoving match and quite by accident his head became the sole occupant of the space into which an Indian club was descending. The hollow thwack as wood met bone was amazingly loud. He went down like a poleaxed steer. There was a lot of rushing around and consternation, but no lasting damage. I was never convicted. However suspicion lay over me for a long time. Thereafter some of the baiting tapered off. Word got around that I had ways of getting even. My relationship with Frog-face changed dramatically; most of the time from then on he gave me a wide berth.

The concert proved to be less than a resounding success. Like everything else that Miss Gaudreau did, her heart was not in it.

The school, a drab frame structure, had few amenities. There was a water bucket and a dipper on a shelf at the back of the room. The water was carried from the town well by the son of the school janitor, an owl-eyed kid in grade five, who watched like a hawk every drink taken. Most everybody drank from the dipper and returned whatever they hadn't drunk back to the bucket. Anyone who didn't want to drink from the dipper fashioned a paper cup from exercise-book paper and filled it with the dipper. The result was the same, they were drinking second-hand water anyway.

There were two toilets—girls and boys. They stood in a thicket of saskatoon bushes at the bottom of an icy slope at the back door. Neither had a door. Both had Eaton's or Simpson's catalogues hung on nails beside the one-hole seats. Only dire necessity prompted anyone to sit on the seat in the boy's toilet in winter. The ice encrustation grew—proportionate to the number of kids who couldn't pee down the hole without missing—until, by spring, the entire seat was a slick yellow ice-sheet. The break-up coincided with that of the river, sometime along about April.

There was the school stable where horses were tethered and fed. A few of the kids came on horseback, some riding long distances no matter what the weather. Others came in cutters behind single horses. One family of three had a cutter all closed in with a heater in it. They would head for home with smoke pouring from the pipe on top, that is until one day the whole thing caught fire and they narrowly escaped cremation. Most kids walked. One family of four walked more than three miles each way, carrying frozen sandwiches in lard pails or syrup cans. Most days they were so tired they fell asleep in the warm classroom.

Danny, a small serious kid in grade three, was crying as he sat on the icy school steps huddled up with his back to the wind. Everybody had left. Ernie and I were late getting out.

"What's the matter, Danny?" I asked.

"My horse . . . it's dead." He sobbed, his face buried in his coat sleeve.

"Dead! Where. Where is it?"

He pointed to the stable. We walked over. It was dead, all right, lying flat on its side, the saddle still on its back. It had been a nice little horse, and Danny had loved it. Why it had died was anyone's guess, and an autopsy would never be performed.

"What are you gonna do, Danny?" we asked.

"I gotta go home. I gotta walk, I guess. My dad is gonna be mad."

It would be plenty dark before he got home. It was long way to walk all alone. And in the dark, the black muskeg spruce took on scary shapes. We watched him go: a little kid walking into the gloom of a winter night, a kid who after a long lonely walk, would have to explain to his father why his horse had died.

He walked for the rest of the winter.

The man who ran the livery barn came the next day, hooked a team of horses onto the stiff body of the little black horse and skidded it away, somewhere to where the coyotes would find it. The saddle hung in the stable until spring when somebody came to collect it. Danny never did get another horse.

By comparison, we were fortunate. We lived within a five minute walk of the school.

With spring came baseball or the game of scrub. Baseball needed teams; scrub didn't. We played before school, at recess and noon-hour on muddy school grounds. There was a considerable slope to the ground, and a fair hit was a home-run, since the ball would keep going downhill to the road and, with any luck, the railroad tracks beyond.

And then there was fighting. Having moved from the hallways and cloakrooms to the outside, we were not under the watchful eye of Mr. Milhausen, and feuds that had simmered all winter flared into open fisticuffs. Owen and I were not always involved, but we took our share of lumps. We also made friends. There were those whose interests lay in other things than warfare and with them we founded friendships.

The end of June came and with it the end of the school year. The exams were no trouble, and Miss Gaudreau finally had to let me out of grade two. I was twelve by then.

When September rolled around, there was a change of teachers. Miss Gaudreau had gone off somewhere and got married; I never saw her again. Mr. Milhausen went farming. The last time I saw him, he looked almost happy.

10 • Never Deal with Snakes

THERE'S A DESERT SHOW IN TOWN," SAID FATHER, BETWEEN BITES of cold roast beef.

"What kind of a show is a desert show?" Mother asked.

"I think it's just some guy with a tent full of snakes, but I haven't seen it. Gus told me about it."

Owen and I looked at each other across the breadth of the oilcloth-covered table. Father caught the look.

"Forget it. You two get home here after school. There's chores to do, and you both know it."

"If you hurry and get your work done . . . " Mother's voice trailed off.

"What kind of snakes are they, poisonous ones, like rattlesnakes, maybe?" Owen asked.

"I told you I haven't seen them. Never mind about them, just eat your lunch. And get a pail of water before you go back to school."

"And the woodbox needs filling too," Mother added.

The tent was there all right. Despite Father's injunction, we didn't go straight home after school. We had to see if there really was a tent and where. At recess we talked about the desert show.

"There's snakes in there eight feet long," Jimmy Donahue said, "with big fangs that stick up, and they spit poison."

"Were you in there already?"

"No, but the guy told me. He said it would be open after

147

school. He didn't want anybody in before that. He said the snakes were sleeping."

"Yeeah! . . . snakes don't sleep."

"That's what the guy said."

"How much to get in?"

"Twenty-five cents."

"Wow! that much, eh."

Yes, the tent was there, a big grimy-looking bell tent on the weed-grown lot beside the skating rink. We swung around through back alleys, avoiding the front window of Father's office on the off chance he might be in it, unlikely though that was; at that time in the afternoon he was usually in the beer parlour, but we weren't taking any chances.

A big sign, painted on canvas and stretched between two posts, proclaimed that what was inside was the biggest and best show of live reptiles, curiosities, and desert denizens to be seen anywhere in the world. Something for the whole family to enjoy, all for the modest price of twenty-five cents—babies free.

There was nobody coming or going. Provocative though the advertising was, the townsfolk weren't exactly knocking themselves out to get there.

"Well, now! Hello there, boys, come to see the show, have you? A great show we've got here. You're the first. C'mon in."

The author of the invitation was short and shaped somewhat like his tent. His dress did not indicate prosperity; a desert show was obviously not a lucrative venture. A faded chequered shirt with a torn collar, almost as dirty as the tent, covered his thick upper body. It disappeared into the top of a pair of choke-bore trousers that were hoisted high into his crotch by a pair of wide-striped suspenders, leaving insufficient leg length to meet the tops of his rundown boots. Through the gap I could see he wasn't wearing any socks, and there was a dirty ring on his ankles where the leather rubbed.

His words were friendly and he was smiling, but it was a cold kind of smile; a snake's smile, I thought.

"Walter here will take your money and show you inside. You've all got twenty-five cents, haven't you?"

Walter was standing at the tent flap, an apron with a pocket on the front tied around his middle. He was a skinny kid, bigger than us . . . maybe sixteen, rangy and hungry-looking. He had a tweed cap pulled down over his forehead and his narrow rabbit face peered out from under it. He held out his hand.

We looked at each other.

"How much for kids?" Jimmy Donahue piped up. Jimmy usually had more money than the rest of us and he was more inclined to speak up too. He was kind of mouthy, people said, but then he didn't have a father to shut him up, and his mother was sort of sickly so she let him get away with a lot of things.

"Twenty-five cents, like the sign says. Just give it to Walter, there, and he'll let you in."

We moved away a little and into a huddle, looking past the fat guy at Walter, who was guarding the entry.

"We don't have any money," Owen and I said together, looking at Jimmy. "How about loaning us some?"

"I only got thirty-five cents."

"Maybe if we go around back, we can sneak in under the tent," Owen said.

I had visions of coming face to face with an eight-foot long rattlesnake spitting poison, if I poked my head under that canvas sidewall.

"Not me," I said.

There wasn't much chance of getting past Walter and the fat guy without paying. Neither looked too benevolent. Walter looked like he could be mean, and if we did try anything like sneaking under the tent, he would probably nab us. He looked like he could run pretty fast too.

"C'mon, let's go," I said, "Maybe Mom will give us two bits."

"We have to go home and get our money," Owen said to

the fat guy who was watching us with black beady little eyes, like raisins sticking out of a pudding. "We'll be back after awhile."

"That's OK, boys. You just bring your money, and, saay . . . pass the word around, will you? I might be able to give you a deal, if you do that."

"Yeah, OK, we'll do that . . . for sure."

It was warm for October. Owen and I sat on the wood pile watching the sun dip behind the fairgrounds and talked about snakes. Tomorrow was Saturday, and somehow, we were going to get into that tent.

It wasn't going to be in the morning.

"There's potatoes to dig," said Father. "It could turn cold any day, now, so you two get busy."

"If you work hard this morning," Mother said, "I'll give you enough money to go to the desert show this afternoon."

Father's face clouded.

"They don't need to be paid for everything they do around here. They should be damn glad to have potatoes . . ."

Mother was as used to this kind of ranting as we were. She was unperturbed.

"It's educational. It will be good for them to see something like that. I've never seen a desert show . . . not that I'm all that keen on snakes, but . . ."

"Well, there better be a lot of spuds out of the ground . . ." Father was loath to concede anything.

We dug. There was no way we were going to get them all out in one morning, but we were not taking any chances on Father nixing the deal either. We worked hard, turning over the heavy clay with spading forks.

"You can't go looking like that." Mother looked distastefully at our overalls, the fronts well plastered with potato-patch earth. "Wash your hands and faces, and put on some clean clothes."

Later, we handed Walter our money and eased through the flap.

Even though it was the middle of the day the inside of the tent was cool and gloomy; the dirty canvas didn't let in much sunlight.

I wasn't sure what I expected of a desert show: a stage with performers perhaps? Maybe Arabs with camels? I don't know. However, it was none of those. A canvas wall, waist-high on us, divided off about a third of the tent. Inside this enclosure was obviously where the attraction was. I looked over the top, and at first I didn't see anything, just trampled weeds and bare ground. Then something moved, a slow sinuous movement, and I became aware of a dry rattling like seeds in a pod. Hey! there were real rattlesnakes in there, none of them eight-feet long, though. Coiled the way they were, even the biggest would have fit on a pie plate. They were the same colour as the weeds and the dusty earth and were hard to see. There were six all coiled up and a couple stretched out.

"Them straight guys is bull snakes. I seen them before," said a tall cowboy-looking guy who had followed us in. "They ain't poisonous."

Owen and I stood leaning over the canvas, looking and waiting for something to happen, like one of the rattlesnakes spitting poison or something, but they just lay there doing nothing.

"Aren't they going to do anything?" Owen asked the fat guy who was leaning against a post in the corner of the enclosure.

"It's pretty cool in here, they're kind of torpid."

"What's 'torpid'?"

"Snakes like warmth. When it's cool they don't move around much."

"Can't you make them do something, like spit poison or show their fangs or something?"

The fat guy reached over the barrier and picked up a wooden apple box. He advanced toward a snake that had shown some semblance of life and swung the box, missing its

head by about a foot. It recoiled and its rattling became more
agitated. He swung again. The snake struck, launching itself
at the box, but missing. The fat guy swung again and the
snake struck, but with less enthusiasm. The third and fourth
times he swung, he got no reaction. The rattling continued,
but the reptile effectively said "to hell with it" and withdrew
its head into its coils and sulked.

"Is that all it's going to do?" somebody asked.

"Like I said, they're torpid. They don't move much."

We could only look so long at something that wasn't doing
anything, and then we started casting around for the other
attractions. There weren't many. In the rear of the tent was a
wooden table. On it was a big glass jar containing an amor-
phous mass floating in a yellowish liquid. The label, printed
in childish letters, said that it was a two-headed calf pre-
served in alcohol, the only one to be seen in the world.

"Hey! lookit the two-headed calf," said Owen. "What's a
two-headed calf got to do with the desert, eh?"

"What's in there?" asked Jimmy, peering into a low wood-
en box partially filled with gravel. "I don't see nothing."

"Them is horned toads," said Walter, coming up behind us.
"They live in the desert."

"They look like a couple of dried up cow chips," Jimmy
said. "What are they supposed to do, eat flies?"

"Don't get smart with me," Walter said, giving Jimmy a
mean look.

We wandered back to the snake pen. A few people had
come in and the fat guy was trying to make the snakes strike
at the apple box again. He wasn't having much success. There
was some mumbling about gyppo desert shows.

We left the gloom of the tent for the sunshine outside. At
least I've seen a rattlesnake and I've seen one strike, I
thought, feeling somewhat dissatisfied otherwise.

During the night the western Alberta weather showed the
other side of its face; in the morning there was two inches of
snow lying on everything and the temperature had dropped

below freezing. After Sunday school we wandered down by the skating rink. Cold weather automatically made us think about skating. The dirty bell tent was still there, sagging under the weight of snow. A stove pipe was sticking out of the flap and a thin thread of smoke was issuing from it. The fat guy, wearing a toque and a ragged sweater, was chopping wood outside. I didn't see Walter anywhere.

"Hey, mister, did your snakes freeze?" Owen asked.

"No, but I have to keep the fire going or they will."

"What do you feed them?" I asked.

"Not much. Mice mostly, but they haven't been fed for awhile. I don't have any mice."

"If we set some mouse traps, we might be able to catch a couple."

"They won't eat dead mice. They gotta be alive."

He took a couple of swings with the axe.

"Look, if you kids want to catch some live mice, I'll pay you for them, but they gotta be alive, mind you."

"How much are you paying?"

"I'll give you four cents apiece if they're in good shape."

We stopped by Jimmy's house on the way home.

"You want to make some money, Jim? If we can find some mice, the fat guy will buy them off us for four cents apiece. Do you know where we could catch some, maybe? They gotta be alive, though."

"Stooks. There's always mice under stooks."

"Hey! Gibson's got lots of stooks, down by the river in his field. We could get mice under them I bet," said Owen.

He was right.

The stooks, each made from eight big bundles of oats still waiting to be thrashed, marched in neat rows across the twenty-acre field bordered on two sides by the river. The snow that capped them would melt in a few days; winter hadn't really come yet. We started taking them apart, bundle by bundle, the mice retreating as the stook got smaller until when the last sheaf was lifted, there was a mad scramble for cover.

We flopped on top of them, grabbing with our mittened hands and popping them into jam cans and lard pails with holes punched in the lids. Most stooks had mice under them. Some got away, but as the afternoon wore away the cans became satisfyingly heavy with seething furry masses. Line after line of stooks fell, the bundles lying wherever they were thrown, haphazard tangles of wet sheaves.

We were wet, cold and muddy when we stopped at the tent, but we had livestock to sell.

"We've got enough mice to feed all your snakes and some left over for tomorrow," I said to the fat guy.

He looked a little dubious.

"How many have you got?"

"Forty-three. Some are bigger than others. There's a couple of great big ones," I said.

"Forty-three, eh! That's a lot. Let's see—now, how much will that be?" At four cents apiece . . ." His lips moved and he counted on his fingers.

"I figure that comes to about eighty cents. Right?"

"Hey! No," we all said.

"That comes to a dollar, seventy-two," said Jimmy.

"A dollar seventy-two?" He got a far away look in his eyes, and again he counted carefully on his fingers whispering the numbers as he did so.

He nodded, finally.

"A little slip-up there, boys, but you're right, and a deal is a deal."

He reached in his pocket and brought out a few coins.

"Look, I only got ninety-five cents. If you want, I can pay you that right now and we'll call it square, or I can go to the bank in the morning and you can come around tomorrow after school and I'll pay you the whole thing. What do you say?"

We looked at each other. Ninety-five cents split three ways wasn't as good as a dollar seventy-two split three ways.

"We can come back after school tomorrow," I said, and the others nodded agreement.

We turned to go.

"Well now . . . How about leaving the mice. Them snakes have been looking forward to their supper. You wouldn't take them away, now, would you?"

"Yeah, I guess we can leave them."

We handed him the cans.

"Good. I knew you boys would feel sorry for them snakes. They're pretty cold and hungry. I'll see you tomorrow. Don't forget . . . right after school."

"Where on earth have you two been?" said mother, as we came in the house. "You're filthy and wet and on Sunday too! Get those clothes off before you get against anything."

Our explanation didn't exactly mollify her, but the fact that we had earned some money took the edge off.

Nobody talked much about the desert show next morning at school. Most had seen it, and most thought it was kind of a gyp. We didn't say anything about our business with the fat guy, just in case others got the idea that there was money in live mice.

As soon as school was out, we headed for the lot beside the skating rink. I had figured out a couple of things I would spend the money on.

"Hey! The tent's gone," Owen said.

A bare earth ring, exactly the size of the tent and surrounded by melting snow, was all there was left.

"Maybe he moved," I said.

"Where would he go?"

"I don't know."

"I'm gonna ask," Jimmy said, walking over to the garage. We followed.

"That guy? He packed up and left ...about ten o'clock this morning," said Ray, bringing his head up out of the Essex 'super six' he was working on. "He piled everything, snakes and all, on that old truck of his and him and Walter took off. Why? It wasn't much of a show. If you didn't see it, you didn't miss much."

"He owes us a bunch of money," Jimmy said. "He was supposed to pay us after school."

"What did he owe you guys money for?"

"We caught a bunch of mice for him, for his snakes to eat."

"So you're the ones, eh!"

"What do you mean?"

"There's a lot of Gibson's stooks lying flat; somebody knocked them over. I heard that the police are interested. They want to know who did it."

"Nah."

"You wait and see."

Constable Bone was tall and looked as hard as his name implied. I had once heard Joe Fortin say, "That bugger would arrest his own mother."

He was waiting outside the school the next afternoon, all squeaking leather and shining buttons. I couldn't help staring at the huge holstered pistol attached to his belt. What was scarier, though, was that Father was with him. He crooked his finger at us as we came out.

"You too, Donahue," he said.

"You boys been catching mice?" Bone inquired.

"Yeah, I guess so," we kind of mumbled.

"How many did you get?"

"Forty-three, all together, but . . ."

"How much was the guy going to pay you?"

"Four cents apiece, but . . ."

"Did he pay you?"

"No. He never. Him and Walter took off and . . . he never . . ."

"That's too bad. You see, those mice belonged to Mr. Gibson, so now I guess you boys owe him a dollar seventy-two."

I couldn't believe what I was hearing.

"We never got paid, we haven't got any money." I looked at Father. He seemed unconcerned. He was gazing off toward the United church.

"There's also the matter of a bunch of stooks that need to

be stood up again," Constable Bone said. "Mister Gibson would like them stood up right away so they will dry out."

"But we have to dig potatoes."

"That is your problem. Mr. Gibson's problem is a bunch of wet oat sheaves."

"But when can we do it, the stooking I mean?"

"Today is Tuesday. I will be back on Thursday. Mr. Gibson and I will have a look in his field on Thursday afternoon. All of those sheaves had better be stooked. You understand?"

We understood.

"If the stooks are all made properly and don't fall down, Mr. Gibson may—he just may—waive payment for the mice."

The constable took off his stiff-brimmed scout hat and eased himself into his Hudson. Father went around the other side and opened the door.

"You two get home, change your clothes and start stooking," he said across the top of the car. "And Donahue, you get busy too."

Jim was about to say something, probably something lippy, but Bone looked at him through the car window, his cold blue eyes drilling right through Jim's skinny body and out the other side.

We stooked until it was pretty dark. The snow had mostly melted and the sheaves were heavy as lead. I couldn't believe we had knocked over so many.

Jim was dogging it a bit.

"Your old man can't tell me what to do. He's not my boss,"

"The guy with the big gun is your boss though. We'll just tell him you wouldn't help stook. Maybe he'll throw you in jail. Or maybe he'll just pull out that gun and bam! . . ."

After supper I was ready to sit down and read a Doc Savage magazine.

"All right," said Father. "You light the lanterns. There's wood to get in, water to carry, and then you can both dig potatoes until bedtime."

"Dig potatoes at night?"

"Yes, and be sure you get them all out of the ground."

Wednesday was the same. I began to worry that we weren't going to get all of the stooks stood up by Thursday afternoon. We worked hard. I guess Jim began to worry a bit too. He pitched in.

It was getting on toward dark on Thursday when we finished. Constable Bone and Gibson hadn't shown up.

"Maybe we better stop at Gibson's and tell him we're finished, eh?"

"Yeah, I guess so."

Mrs. Gibson came to the door.

"Is Mr. Gibson home?" I asked.

"Yes. Matter of fact, he's just got home. He's been in Edmonton for the last ten days. He's just got home a few minutes ago. I'll get him."

We looked at each other. What we had heard began to sink in a bit.

Mr. Gibson was a tall man. He stood looking down at us. Inquiring.

"What can I do for you boys?"

"We just wanted to tell you that we got all of your stooks back up."

"Were there many down?"

"Yeah, quite a few."

"I didn't know. Must have been the snow. I've been away in Edmonton, you know. I'm glad you boys stood them back up. How much do I owe you?"

"Owe us?"

"Yeah. It's worth something to me to get those sheaves up out of the wet. Here . . . How about a buck apiece?"

I guess our mouths were hanging open. Owen and I couldn't think of anything to say right off and for once Jim seemed tongue-tied.

Gibson handed us a dollar each.

"Thanks, boys. Now you better go and get those wet clothes off."

He closed the door.

"What are we gonna tell Father?" Owen asked.

"I dunno."

Jim didn't have too much to worry about, or did he? Us? Well, I had a lot of thinking to do before I got home.

11 • A Bad Flue

I WAS THIRTEEN THAT SPRING, EXPECTED TO WORK LIKE A MAN AND behave like a boy, while being neither one.

All last fall and through the winter, Father had been renovating an old house—actually, two old houses put together to make one. It would eventually become our home and get us out of the rented place we were in. Father was not a very good carpenter, but he had gotten the two buildings put together after a fashion and was down to finishing the inside. Whenever he needed help, which seemed to me to be most of the time, I was commandeered. I hadn't minded much during the spring, but here it was, early summer, school was out and the river with its quiet eddies and sandy beaches beckoned.

We had reached the stage when the chimney had to be built. Never before had we had a brick chimney on any house we had ever lived in, just tin stovepipes sticking up through the roof. Father was determined that in this one we would have a proper chimney.

He had bought the bricks and lime and had a pile of sand dumped in the yard by the door. All he needed was a bricklayer. He had conceded that it was enough to be a bad carpenter without being a bad bricklayer too.

The only person around who had any bricklaying credentials at all was Seamus O'Flaherty. He was also known as the town drunk. However because he was a World War veteran he was, like all war veterans, a friend of father's and regardless of his masonry talents, the one to consider. Logic to the contrary, Father hired him.

I had known Seamus for a long time. All of us kids had cadged nickels and dimes off him when he was too drunk to know what he was doing. I was flabbergasted when Father said he was going to build our chimney. That he could build anything was beyond belief.

"I want you to stay around tomorrow and give old Seamus a hand," he had said. "I won't be back until late afternoon and somebody has to keep an eye on him."

"You mean he's actually going to build a chimney for us?" I asked, not quite ready to believe what I was hearing. "Does he know how?"

"He knows how." Father seemed quite confident. "He was a bricklayer in the old country before he went to sea. He knows how to build a chimney."

"What time is he coming?" I asked, a lack of enthusiasm in my voice and I guess showing on my face as well.

"Early," said Father, "and you can take that look off your face. I want you over there by eight o'clock and stay there until he's done. It's not a big job. It probably won't take all day."

So there I was, on a silky clean morning with fat yellow sunlight lying on everything, waiting for Seamus to show up.

There was no breeze and it would be hot later on, a good reason to be anywhere else preferably down by the river.

I leaned back against the warm tarpaper wall and gradually let my feet slide out until I was sitting on the boardwalk that led from the gate to the front door.

The train whistle blew for the crossing, that made it nine o'clock. I waited. I listened to the bees on the saskatoon blossoms and I watched ants march across the toes of my boots. After an hour there was still no Seamus.

I watched Alec, a lean elderly bachelor who lived across the road, split firewood. He worked for awhile and then stuck his axe in the chopping block and climbed onto his porch. He went inside, left the door open, turned the radio on real loud, and came out. He bent his tall spare figure into his porch chair, tilted it on its spindly back legs against the wall and hooked his feet in the rungs just as the ten o'clock news came on.

The air was beginning to dance in the rising heat. Sitting there was fine, but I was getting sick of doing nothing. I kept looking up the road and wishing Seamus would get there. On the other hand, I was sort of hoping he wouldn't come at all. I bet myself that he wasn't going to show up.

The news was over and the grain and cattle prices came on. I would wait until they were finished and then I would leave. I killed a few flies that had congregated on the warm tarpaper wall by squishing them with a piece of lumber.

His head appeared first, bobbing above the brow of the hill, then his body elongated until his entire stubby figure, distorted by the heat devils, rose over the crest. He came toward me down the sloping roadway, with the rolling gait of a seafaring man.

It seemed that the wind was hard on his beam; he was heeled well-over and making way to leeward. He almost fetched up in the portside ditch, caught himself in time and tacked to starboard, narrowly missing grounding on the rocks surrounding the neighbour's flower garden. He steered an erratic course down the slight grade until, seeing me waiting by the gate, he hove-to and stood there puffing and peering at me, trying to bring my face into focus and bathing me in the combined effluvia of beer, onions, and unwashed clothes.

I might have known. He had waited for the beer parlour to open and had downed a few to fortify himself against the rigours of the day's work.

He was about five feet high—not much taller than me—a bandy-legged gnome in the best storybook sense. It was hard to tell how old he was, but I knew he had to be in his early fifties. His face, a map of Ireland, carried several scars and was mottled from a long association with John Barleycorn. A purple knob of a nose, crazed with blue veins, protruded from several days growth of grey whiskers that hung like moss from his jowls. Above it, peering out from recesses deep under the eaves of a pair of bushy eyebrows—one swept up and the other down—were watery blue eyes.

A chunk of his lower lip was missing, carried away, I was told, by a piece of German shrapnel during a long ago battle somewhere on the high seas. From this hole protruded a soggy home-rolled cigarette, tobacco tendrils leaking from the end.

His shirt, blue- and white-striped and dirty, had once had a collar attached by a stud at the back. It was tucked into what had been in better days, dress pants, now of indeterminate colour and stained down his leg where he had wet himself. They were stretched dangerously over a round beer belly. His fly was undone, the buttons gone. On one side, his galluses had come adrift and the loose rigging trailed behind.

Crowning his diminutive figure, pulled down to his ears, rode a bowler hat, sweat-stained and grimy.

"Good morning, Mister O'Flaherty." I said.

"Good morning, is it then?" came a wheezing reply.

"Yes, Sir," I said.

"And you'll be the one who's to help me, I suppose," was more of a statement than a question. The exertion of speaking brought on a fit of coughing.

"I am," I said. "What would you like me to do?"

"To do, Bhoy? I'm the one who's to do, you're the one who's to help me." With that he pushed past me and wove the few short steps along the path to the door. He paused to give a cursory glance at the pile of bricks waiting for him and then entered what was to be our living room and from where the chimney would arise. I followed, not knowing what to say next.

We had built a platform inside against the living-room wall, some six or seven feet from the floor. From it, the chimney would begin its ascent to the roof and its eventual destination about four feet higher than the ridge. It was common practice to build chimneys on platforms. To start at foundation level would take almost twice as many bricks, and bricks were expensive. All told, there was to be about nine feet of chimney.

Above the platform was a square hole cut in the roof. Under the platform, we had knocked together a scaffold and a ladder leading to it out of scrap lumber. We had also made a board for mixing mortar on. It occupied the middle of the floor.

Seamus stood there wheezing, leaning against the scaffold. He peeked up through the hole in the roof and winced as though the light was too bright. He glanced about, seemingly disappointed that everything was ready to go.

He backed up to a sawhorse and hoisted himself with some difficulty onto it. He sat looking vacantly at the room, his feet in laceless run-over leather boots, swinging free of the floor.

I stood dithering. I had some doubts that Seamus was in fit condition to do anything, but if he was I wanted him to get on with it.

"The sand, Bhoy, where's the sand . . . and the lime, we'll need lime, you know."

I pointed to the bags of lime leaning against the wall behind him.

"The sand is outside, a big pile. Do you want me to bring some in?" I asked. He glanced at the lime and sighed, which brought on another coughing spell that jettisoned his cigarette across the room.

He fumbled through his pockets and discovered a slim leather pouch. Removing a cigarette paper from the pack within, he attached it by a corner to the dampness of his lip. Studiously measuring out a pinch of tobacco—losing some onto the floor, his hand was shaking so badly—he moulded it in his palm, retrieved the paper from his lip and with great deliberation fashioned another lumpy-looking cigarette. With trembling hands he elevated it to meet his tongue, carefully licked the glued edge, smoothed it between his fingers, and nestled it in the hole in his lip.

He applied the flame from a huge wooden match to the brushy end of his hand-crafted masterpiece, inhaled a great lungful of smoke and almost expired. His face turned blue and his cough rasped upward from somewhere near his midriff.

"Would you by chance have any trowels, Bhoy?" he asked when his coughing bout subsided and he could recommence breathing. "Mine's got mislaid, somewhere."

"We have two," I said, "a big one and a little one." I got the trowels from the toolbox in the corner.

"Are these all right?"

He hefted them, turned them over, tapped one against the other. The musical clang seemed to satisfy him.

"They're fine. Not as good as mine, mind you, but they're fine."

At this juncture, he seemed to entertain some vague thought of doing something. Perhaps I was showing too much eagerness standing there in front of him because he fixed me with a sour look, squinting through the smoke curling up past his eye. He shifted his weight on the sawhorse as though to stand, then thought better of it and subsided.

"The sand, Bhoy, why are you not bringing in the sand?"

"How much do you want?" I asked.

"Never mind your asking questions," he said, "just bring the sand. I'll tell you when there's enough."

I got a bucket and filled it at the sand pile, brought it in and dumped it on the mixing board. I looked at him, but before I got the question out, he waved his hand signalling more. I brought more, three more buckets full. As I dumped the last one, he looked critically at the pile.

"That will do, Bhoy, now where's the lime?"

I opened a bag and poured out a bucketful, dumped it on the sand and glanced at him.

"Enough, Bhoy, now some water. You have to have water to make mortar you know. You should know that, Bhoy."

I brought a bucket of water from the rain barrel.

"Mix the sand and lime first," he said. "Then pour on the water. Has nobody ever show'd you how to mix mortar . . . and here they said you were a bright lad and you don't know the first thing about mixing mortar."

I shovelled the pile, turning it over until the sand and lime took on a uniform grey colour.

"Now the water, not too much to start."

After grumbling and the addition of small quantities of water, the mortar achieved a consistency to his liking. So far, he had done nothing more useful than direct my activities, cough, and puff on his cigarette.

"Enough, Bhoy . . . now the bricks. Bring them in and stack them within my reach and be quick. We don't have all day to do a small job like this. Your father will be asking why it's taking so long."

I carried bricks, an armload at a time and stacked them on the scaffold.

"Now then, when I get up on the scaffold, you'll hand me the mortar," he said, indicating a wide piece of board I was to put it on.

He dismounted the sawhorse and started up the ladder. At the third rung his foot went between the horizontals and he let out a groan as his leg went through to the crotch.

"Ahhhh. . . Bhoy, t'is hard on the jewels," he gasped. He wheezed and his face distorted. I was alarmed, but in a moment he extricated himself and crawled the remaining rungs to the platform where he sat rocking back and forth, a pained expression on his face.

I hoisted a board full of mortar to him and, after working it with the trowel and grumbling, he smeared some on a brick and placed it on the platform. At last—I had given up any hope of finishing early.

He puffed and groaned with every movement. His cigarette

had been extinguished by the moisture being wicked along its length, but it retained its position in the hole in his lip. He knelt on the scaffold and this constricted position seemed to affect his digestive process since it elicited from him frequent loud farts.

"Ha, Bhoy, t'was a good one," he commented after each.

As the column began to grow I began to doubt that it and the aperture above would meet head on. We had built the platform rather roomy with the idea being to box the whole affair in at some time in the future. Seamus had started laying bricks without due reference to the hole.

I was in a quandary. At thirteen years old, one did not offer to correct the endeavors of grown-ups. My relationship with Seamus was not one where I felt confident to offer advice.

"Mr. O'Flaherty," I finally said, "would you like me to get you a square or a level? We have both and we have a plumb-bob in the tool box."

"Never you bother, Bhoy, t'will not be necessary. They'll only get in the way. Your time will be better spent bringing more bricks. As you can see, I'll be needing them soon."

Within a foot and a half of the opening, he must have realized "that the twain were never to meet." He said not a word, but the bricks began to show a decided offset, journeying in quest of a route to the roof.

When the last course of bricks that could be laid from the inside had been squeezed into place, the upper reaches had taken on a neat staircase effect not seen on most chimneys.

Seamus studied the face of a huge turnip of a pocket-watch, attached by a black shoelace to a belt loop on his pants. "T'is time for me dinner," he said, belching at the prospect. "While I'm gone, you'll be getting bricks to the roof, and mind you don't fall off."

"When will you be back?" I asked.

"When I've had me dinner, when else? Bhoy. You ask the most foolish questions."

I ran home the few blocks to the house we were renting,

gulped down a sandwich and a glass of milk, fearful that Seamus would be back before I got some bricks on the roof.

I needn't have worried . . .

Our ladder, made from two-by-fours, was leaning against the house. Like everything Father made, it was strong but ugly. I couldn't even move it by myself. On the ridge near the chimney hole, we had made a platform for holding bricks and mortar.

It wasn't easy negotiating the ladder with bricks in my hands and it took a good many trips before I had a decent pile. Seamus had still not returned. I mixed a new batch of mortar and carried some in a pail to the platform. Still no Seamus.

I waited on the roof. The sun was at its zenith and a blue heat haze had built on the surrounding hills. It was hot sitting in the glare reflected off the new shingles. I was becoming fearful that the mortar would congeal and I would have to make another batch.

He eventually arrived, if not in a jovial mood certainly more affable than he had been earlier in the day. I don't know what or how much he had eaten, but it was obvious that he had not neglected his liquid intake. Sitting on the peak of the roof, I had a longer view of the road and had seen his approach from further off. His progress was, if anything, more erratic than it had been in the morning.

"Ah . . . there's a good lad," he said, displaying the first sign of approbation so far that day; "you've gone an' got a few bricks up, have you? Well, we'll soon make short work of them."

He started up the ladder. It was all of fifteen feet from the ground to the eaves, the ground on that side of the house having a decided slope to it. About half way, he seemed to run out of steam. He paused, looked down between the rungs then upwards and belched.

"T'is a trifle high, Bhoy, that it is."

Not knowing what to say, I remained silent.

He continued his assault, each step becoming more laborious. He reached the junction of the ladder and the eaves and rested, still clutching the ladder side rails that extended somewhat further up. He surveyed the expanse of the shingled roof in front of him, likening it, I'm sure, to a vast glacial mountain slope still to be negotiated without benefit of rope or crampon.

I had had no trouble going between the ladder and ridge with my rubber-soled shoes. His were worn leather, slick, and without a vestige of tread. He ventured out, took two steps, and his feet went out from under him. He slid back into the V made by the ladder and the roof. Thankfully, he had had the foresight to hang on to the ladder.

"Why are you sitting there, Bhoy? T'is help I'm needing. Can't you see that, Bhoy?"

I walked down the roof.

"Give me your hand," I said. "Maybe if I pull on you, you'll be able to get up."

"Pull on me, indeed. T'will take more than pulling. T'will be my doom if I fall off, you know. Be a good lad and get some bits of board and a few nails and a hammer. You know how to nail, do you not? Well, nail a few slats to the roof. You should know how to do that, Bhoy."

I gathered up an armful of scrap and with a hammer protruding from my hip pocket and a handful of nails in my side pocket, I ascended the ladder to where Seamus was still wedged between it and the roof.

"Ahh . . . there's a good Bhoy, we'll make a useful lad out of you yet," he said. "Now nail them about two feet apart all the way up the roof, and mind you drive the nails all the way in."

I did as I was bidden, Seamus grunting approval as each step was nailed firmly in place.

He reached out, clutched the first step and pulled on it, testing the soundness of its attachment to the roof. He then gingerly hauled himself out of his wedge until he could kneel, and on hands and knees ascended the steps to the ridge. He parked himself on a corner of the platform and only then did he dare cast his eyes further than his immediate surroundings. He let out a sigh and reached for his tobacco pouch.

The chimney rose through the roof hole and continued upwards. It began taking on a Pisan appearance in that it had a decided lean, northwards, possibly provoking speculation that the bricks contained quantities of ferrous metal and were being acted upon by the magnetic pole.

He fashioned the flashing out of tin, cursing as he nicked his hands on the sharp edges. We wouldn't know until it rained, how effective it would be.

He said little, laid bricks furiously, pausing only to discard the soggy remains of his cigarettes and roll a replacement. He groaned, puffed, belched, swore, and farted the afternoon away, sweat running off him in rivulets. I was hard pressed to keep him supplied with bricks and mortar, it being a difficult task getting them to the roof.

I said nothing about the deviation from plumb that, if not corrected, would be obvious to anyone passing and, knowing our townsfolk, would become a conversation piece.

"Hey! have you seen Jones' crooked chimney?" I could just hear them saying it. I would take a ribbing, I knew that.

As the afternoon waned his pace quickened. Bits of mortar flew like chaff from a threshing machine and the bricks began to take on a look of the haphazard as he plopped them into the cement with little correction.

I began to be apprehensive of Father's reaction when he came to have a look. Somehow I felt guilty and was certain that I would share some of the blame although it escaped me how I could possibly have intervened to keep the chimney's upward progress vertical.

I began looking toward the direction from which Father would appear, as the shank end of the afternoon drew near. Seamus was now working at breakneck speed, applying the finishing bricks and forming the cap.

"T'will need some pointing," he said, squirming backward along the ridge and surveying his handy work.

"You'll know how to do that, won't you, Bhoy?"

I didn't, but I suspected that whatever pointing was would be a lot of work and I would be slated to do it. It was obvious that it would need considerable finishing if it was to take on the look common to most chimneys. The mortar had squished out from between the bricks in quantity—Seamus's accelerated pace had not allowed for tidying it up—and had solidified, hanging in great ridges and giving the chimney a pagoda-like appearance. Unfortunately, no amount of pointing was going to correct the lean. Even now, the mortar was set and a complete rebuild would be called for if it was ever to assume a perpendicular stance.

"There it is, Bhoy, as done as ever it will be," he said. "The smoke will find it a jhoy climbing up such a chimney."

"Are you all finished?" I asked. "Is that the way you're going to leave it . . . just like that?"

"Indeed I am, Bhoy, Indeed I am. T'will be closing time and I'll not be there, unless I hurry."

He dropped the trowel and squirmed off the platform.

Backwards he went, down the roof, cautiously feeling for each step. He clutched the ladder and gingerly made his way down, grunting and sighing. I followed.

"Will you be back tomorrow?" I asked.

"There'll be no need, there's nought but a bit of finishing . . . and you'll do that, will you not, Bhoy?"

As he stood at the base of the ladder knocking mortar from his clothes with his hat, Father came over the brow of the hill and strode down the road. I could see him eyeing the chimney. Seamus turned and with surprising agility scampered through the garden gate and up the road to meet him.

"Ah . . . you're just in time, Jack, just in time," he said, clutching Father's sleeve and arresting his progress.

"The Bhoy—and a good lad he is—and myself have just at this very moment finished. If you had come a bit sooner you would have found us hard at work. T'is a chimney you can be proud of."

"That's fine, Seamus," said father, in his "old buddy" type voice, attempting to bypass him and get a better look. "From here it looks like it might lean a bit. Does it? It looks a bit rough, too." Father was a little too far away and the angle was wrong to fully appreciate the magnitude of the deviation.

"T'is nothing, nothing at all to worry about," said Seamus, holding his ground between Father and the house. "The Bhoy, and he is a fine Bhoy and a good worker, will have it right as rain within a few moments in the morning."

Father looked at me. I shrugged. What could I say?

"Now," said Seamus, tugging at Father, "T'is almost closing time, but if we are of a mind we can still make it. But hurry man, and I'll stand the first round out of the magnificent wages you're paying me."

Father was not one to refuse an invitation without giving it due consideration. Said consideration took almost half a minute before complete capitulation. He turned and with Seamus grasping his arm, together they disappeared over the hill, Father took a last look roofwards over his shoulder from the brow. Maybe a leaning chimney didn't bother him that much. It was ugly, but it probably wouldn't fall apart.

I was tired. I cleaned the trowels and put them in the tool box. Today had been a day. Tomorrow? T'was sure to be another, indeed it would.

The river would have to wait; I knew where I would be.

12 • Summer Work

W HOA! WHOA!" FATHER SHOUTED IN DESPERATION. HE HAD forgotten for the moment that the Chev wasn't a team of horses. He was straining at the big wooden steering wheel, hauling on it as if it were reins, trying to get us stopped. He finally remembered the pedals under his feet and jammed his foot down hard on the right one. The brake shoes screamed in protest but gradually took hold and we slid to a halt, slewing sideways, just short of a pool big enough to swallow the whole front end. Getting stuck up to the running boards was a certainty if we continued on; the lane ahead was a quarter of a mile of black mud, rain-filled wheel tracks, and potholes of unknown depth.

"I'll walk the rest of the way," I said and opened the door.

I got out, reached into the back seat, and dragged my suitcase and blanket roll out. I kicked the door shut.

"Goodbye," I said, somewhat at a loss.

I had never gone anywhere by myself before for any length of time and it felt strange having to say goodbye. I stood there awkwardly, feeling that something more was called for.

"Your mother and I will probably drive out tomorrow in the evening," Father said, through the rolled-down window. He looked grave, as though he was sending me off to war or something. "We'll stop by. She'll want to see how you're getting on. Be a good boy and do as you're told." That admonition came automatically. He was not great on advice, but being an army man, he felt everything would be fine as long as I obeyed orders.

I watched him back the Chev around. He wasn't a very good driver—he had never quite made the transition from horses—and it took him awhile to get it pointed in the opposite direction. The wheels spun as he let the clutch pedal come up too fast, and he went jack-rabbiting toward the main road, mud flying from the rear tires.

I slung my bedroll over my shoulder and with my old club bag bumping my leg, headed up the lane: a wagon track bordered on both sides by saskatoon bushes and barbed wire fences. By walking in the wet grass close to the fence, I kept clear of the worst of the mud in the furrows and water-filled holes that were now black mirrors reflecting the low-angled sun.

The faint grumbling of thunder and a pile of dark clouds low on the eastern horizon were all that remained of the storm that had filled every depression. The evening air was heavy with its passing and thick with the smell of wet earth and clover. From the grass on both sides trickled the call of meadowlarks.

At the end of the lane to the right was the house, a square box covered with unpainted weathered siding, its drabness relieved for the moment by the gold of its west-facing windows. Over to the left loomed the grey bulk of the barn. Between it and the house scattered among pole fences were several ramshackle log buildings. One, larger than the rest, with a rusted tin stovepipe sticking up at an angle and the look of an original homestead house, was the only one that could be the bunkhouse. I decided the rest looked too dilapidated, their backs broken and grass growing out of mossy thatches.

I knew I would probably have to live in a bunkhouse, and had conjured up a romantic notion—from the western-story magazines I had read by the dozen—of what one would look like. I imagined it would be a picturesque place where men in big cowboy hats and high-heeled boots sat around a pot-bellied stove, telling yarns. That's where I would live in the bunkhouse, I thought with satisfaction.

A big yellow and grey mongrel came hollering down the road toward me, quartering back and forth, his great plume of a tail held high. He skidded to a halt, stiff-legged, in front of me. I kept walking and he eased around behind, still grumbling. I let him sniff, ready to clout him with my suitcase if he tried anything. He decided I was no threat and went off to sniff a fence post and refresh his claim to it.

Freiburg came out of the old house as I was scrubbing the mud from my boots on a patch of grass. A big German with a shaved head and mutton-chop whiskers, he walked with a slouch, his thumbs hooked in the shoulder straps of his bib overalls.

"Well, you're here, I see," he said, the guttural still apparent in his speech. He had lived in Canada for a long time, ever since the war, but the German was still there.

"I thought the rain might hold you up. Your father didn't get that old car of yours stuck, eh? It rained pretty hard here. No hail, but it sure rained. Rained like hell for a little while."

"Yeah, it rained pretty hard at home too, but we didn't get stuck. The road was OK, a bit slippery though." I said.

"The hay, the cut stuff, it'll be pretty wet I guess, but we'll be able to rake it tomorrow, if it don't rain anymore."

"Yeah, well, I guess that's why I'm here, to help with the haying," I said. I thought I should say something else, to show that I was eager to go to work, but I couldn't think of anything.

"Well, we sure can use you; we're short-handed. Tomorrow we'll put you to work all right." He nodded and smiled as though there was something secret about haying that he wasn't telling me. "But right now, bring your stuff inside. Ernie's up there. Do you know Ernie?" He turned without waiting for an answer.

There was no longer a door attached to the sagging old

house; only the hinges remained. I followed him through the opening into a low-ceilinged room that was so full of junk that I had to hold my suitcase high in front of me to get through it. Boxes, trunks, tubs full of machine parts and tools covered the floor. An assortment of horse collars—the straw stuffing bursting from cracked leather—and harness hung on the log walls, a dusty jumble of mouldy straps and rusting buckles.

In one corner going almost straight up was a narrow staircase. I followed Freiburg's rear end, pushing my suitcase and bedroll ahead of me into the room above.

There wasn't much light. What there was came from one small window overhung with a tattered lace curtain and cobwebs. In the gloom, all I could make out was a confused mass. There were no side walls just the roof angling steeply up from the floor. Two beds, a double and a cot, their heads shoved against the wall at one end, were the only furnishings. The rest of the room like the one below was filled with junk.

"This here is Ernie," said Freiburg. "He started yesterday."

Ernie heaved himself off the double bed. In the gloom, I hadn't noticed him lying there; he was the same colour as the rumpled bedding. He held out his hand, and we shook. He mumbled something and then coughed.

"What's your name?" Freiburg asked. "I forgot."

"Paul," I said.

"Ernie, this here is Paul. He's starting tomorrow."

Ernie didn't say anything. He slumped back on the bed.

"You can have the cot," Frieburg said. "Me and Ernie sleep in the bed. Make yourself at home." He turned and backed down the stairs.

So this was the bunkhouse.

It was nothing like what I had pictured. Even the worst I could have imagined would have been better than this gloomy spider-infested room. I had never been in a place so devoid of comfort. That anyone would expect me to live in it was beyond belief.

I guess it was the dirt and what might be crawling around in it, that got to me. Not only that, but the smell ... Having just come in from the fresh rain-washed air, the stale odour of old sweat, dirt and decay was overpowering. Everything in this stuffy attic was filthy, overlaid with the grime of years. On the rough board floor were lumps of barnyard dirt cast from countless pairs of muddy boots, ancient paper, husks of dead insects, bits of straw, and grey dust that had lain undisturbed by broom or mop for aeons by the look of it. An assortment of clothing hung, like limp corpses on a gallows tree, on nails driven in the pole rafters. Some of it looked as if it had hung there for a long time, maybe for years. The only bright spot was a calendar, spitted on a nail at the head of the bed. The window, if it could be opened, looked like it never had been. By the amount of dirt clinging to it, it had never been washed either, at least not since it was the farm home and someone lived here. I wanted to leave, go back downstairs and into the clean outdoors.

Ernie continued to lie on the bed, not offering to make conversation. He was a gangling young guy with a narrow face, probably a year or so older than me. A few dark whiskers stuck out of his chin. Long dark greasy hair curled over the collar of his shirt that was torn in a couple of places and stained.

For want of something to do, I unrolled my bedroll over the thin dirty mattress of the cot. There was no pillow, and I had no sheets, just two grey blankets. I took my jacket out of my suitcase and rolled it up. It would have to do to put my head on. I finished and sat bent forward to avoid hitting the underside of the roof.

"What's your last name?" I asked Ernie, who was staring straight up at nothing. "Do you live around here?"

His speech came grudgingly, his tongue loose around the words, forming them with difficulty.

"Sim. My name is Sim. My folks, they live up near

Westlock. Where do you come from?"

"Sangudo," I said. "In town. Have you worked before?"

"Yeah, I been working . . . up on the river drive . . . since the break-up."

"What's that?" I asked, "what's a river drive?"

"Driving logs . . . floating them down river after the ice goes out . . . up on the Askabasta. It's done for this year. I came here. I heard O'Donnel needed somebody . . . "

"What's the Askabasta?" I asked.

"The Askabasta River . . . you know, north of here. Don't you know about the Askabasta River?"

"Oh sure" I said. "Yeah, I know. The Athabaska River."

"Yeah, the Asta . . . yeah." He lapsed into silence, his mouth hanging slack.

I sat, not knowing what else to do. The sun went down and the darkness settled in. Ernie bestirred himself and lit the coal-oil lantern that hung from the ridgepole on a wire. He pulled off his shirt and pants and lay back down on the bed, clad only in his underwear, a suit of cotton long johns grey with dirt. I had never seen underwear so dirty. It made me feel itchy, just looking at it.

I asked about the haying, about O'Donnel, the food, and where we ate at mealtimes. The answers were sparse, doled out one syllable at a time. The river drive was the only thing Ernie was inclined to talk about, so I let him. I hadn't done much that I could talk about.

Freiburg came up the stairs carrying a lard pail full of water. He set it on the floor between the beds.

"If you want a drink in the night, help yourself," he said.

He took off his clothes, down to his underwear; it wasn't much cleaner than Ernie's.

"Time to turn in. We start pretty early. Do you need the light?"

"No," I said. I began taking off my clothes.

He raised the chimney and blew. Suddenly it was black. I crawled in between my blankets. There was creaking from the other bed as Ernie and Freiburg heaved around, getting comfortable.

I wasn't tired. I hadn't got up that early and, apart from getting my stuff together, I hadn't done very much all day. I lay there looking at the faint square that was the window. The sour dirt smell of the mattress came up through the blanket. A couple of mosquitoes found me and sang around my head. I tried to swat them, but in the dark I couldn't connect. Freiburg started to snore, great trumpeting snores interspersed with smacking and chewing. Mice rustled in the junk and ran across the floor, their tiny feet whispering under my bed. From the sounds, the place was alive with them. Something landed on the roof and walked along the ridge. Hard claws raked the shingles—probably an owl. The dog went barking off across the field chasing something, maybe his imagination. I lay there, my eyes wide open.

I thought about being at home in the clean bed I shared with my brother, and I wondered why I was here.

I knew why I was here, of course. Work . . . a summer job haying. Father had got it for me. He knew Bill O'Donnel who owned the place. Between them, they had figured a summer of haying would be good for me.

I had turned fifteen in March. It was now the first of June and I was out of school, never to go back. I had got recommended and didn't have to write exams. I had never had a job that lasted more than a day, but having lived on a farm for the first eleven years of my life and having hung around the livery stable in town, doing odd jobs involving horses, I was pretty sure I could hay. I didn't know how much I was to be paid, and I wouldn't know until I talked to O'Donnel, but I felt rich already.

I didn't know O'Donnel, had never seen him that I knew of. Ernie had said he was away for a couple of days, "taking Missus O'Donnel to Edmonton to the doctor." Freiburg would be running things until he got back.

I knew Freiburg. He had the reputation of not staying long at one thing. A bachelor, he lived in a shack on the outskirts of town, next to the hammer mill that he sometimes operated, grinding anything from pig feed to flour, on demand. I guess business was slow, so he was sharecropping hay for O'Donnel.

I dozed off.

The sun was split on the horizon when I walked with Freiburg to the barn. In the morning quiet, I could hear prairie chickens talking in the young oats down by the creek. Other than a haze lying over the fields the air was clean, all traces of yesterday's storm long gone. It would be hot later on, good haying weather.

I felt light-headed. Every time the dog had barked in the night, or the mice became too active, or Freiburg glugged down water, I had awakened with a start, wondering where I was.

Ernie shambled behind, clumping along in a pair of high-top river-driver's boots, the soles bristling with caulks. His khaki "tin" logger's pants, well impregnated with dirt and pine-pitch, were stagged off at his boot tops. He was carrying a pair of milk pails he'd picked up off the screened-in porch at the rear of the house by the kitchen door. He veered off toward a small corral where a couple of cows stood soaking up the sun.

"Can you milk?" Freiburg asked.

"No," I said. The lie came easy. I knew how to milk. I had milked our cows since I was six years old, but I hated the job. I would rather do anything else.

"Ernie can do the milking then; there's only two cows. We'll feed the horses."

He swung the barn doors open. There was an immediate stamping of hooves, low nickering and the creak of wood as the six big work horses moved in their stalls, twisting their heads around to see us and pawing the straw bedding.

"This will be your team," Freiburg said, pointing at the

left-hand end of the row of stalls. "The black is Betty and the grey is Queen. They're both pretty quiet. Ernie drives Jigs and Tony, there. Don't go too close in back of them, they'll kick your bloody head off." I looked at the dinner-plate size hooves on the pair of blue roans standing in a double stall. I would give them a wide birth. You bet I would.

The third team, Jim and Duchess, a big grey gelding and a chestnut mare, was the one Freiburg drove. Duchess was in a box stall with her foal of a couple of months. I scratched the youngster behind the ears. His coat was still curly.

I pushed hay into the mangers from the feed passage in front while Freiburg doled out a lard pail of oats into each feed box. I patted my team and talked to them, easing up into the stalls beside their big, warm, hard-muscled bodies. The sooner they got to know me the better. There was nothing to tell right now how they would behave. Driving a team was one thing, being responsible for two big mares weighing almost a ton each, feeding, watering, harnessing and generally looking after them was something else. I had never had that much responsibility. The realization began to sink in that I had been hired to do a man's work and from here on, I was going to be treated as a man. I walked a little taller toward the house and breakfast.

Ernie emptied the milk pails into the bowl of the De'Laval cream-separator in the corner of the porch. There was the rancid smell of oil and sour milk about it, and the cracked linoleum under it was caked with dirt and dried milk. I grabbed the handle and cranked. A plump young woman came out of the kitchen and held a pitcher under the cream spout. Her face, partially hidden by a tangle of hair, was puffy with sleep. Her big breasts hung loosely under her soiled house dress as she stooped, and she smelled of perspiration. The jug filled, she took it inside, scuffing along in a pair of dirty, run-down slippers. Through the screen door, I saw her put it on the table.

I let the separator handle go as the milk dwindled to a drip and the mechanism spun down. I washed my hands and face in the basin by the door. The towel was grimy, but I used it anyway, avoiding the middle part.

"Berthe, this is Paul," said Freiburg to the sleepy young woman. "Paul, this is Berthe; she's my niece." Berthe bore but slight resemblance to Freiburg. I could see it only because he had mentioned it. She stood in front of the kitchen stove cooking pancakes and barely acknowledged me. I slid in behind the long oilcloth-covered kitchen table against the wall, on a bench beside Ernie. Freiburg sat at one end. An old hawk-faced man, wearing a straw cowboy hat and leaning on a cane, came limping from another room and eased himself into a chair at the other end, grimacing as he bent himself onto the seat.

"Jack, this is Paul, he's going to give us a hand with the haying," Freiburg said, louder than he normally spoke.

"Yeah . . . where did you come from?" the old man said, scarcely looking at me as he reached out an arthritic arm to spear a fork-full of pancakes.

"He lives in Sangudo," Freiburg hollered, not giving me a chance.

"A town kid. Why in hell do we have to have a town kid? Couldn't you find somebody on a farm? Can he drive horses?" He had a voice to match his appearance, that of a querulous old man. "Can you drive a team of horses?" he asked, fixing me with a skeptical look.

"Yeah, I've driven horses. I lived on a farm," I answered. Rather than commit myself further, I jammed a bunch of pancakes into my mouth. They were doughy in the middle.

"Well, we'll have to see. We'll have to see. Hand me that syrup," he said impatiently. I pushed the syrup toward him.

I didn't know who he was, but he seemed to be someone of importance. Freiburg told me later he was O'Donnel's father, an old cowboy out of Montana.

"Don't worry about him; he doesn't come outside much."

I had trouble getting the harness sorted out and getting

it onto my team. Betty was tall, and she didn't know me so she didn't cooperate. She moved around a lot. Queen was not as tall, but she was a cagey old devil. She did everything from trying to squash me against the stall to nipping me with her teeth and stepping on my feet. Freiburg and Ernie had their teams at the water trough by the time I led mine from the barn.

While they were drinking, I had a good look at them. Betty, the younger of the two, was a nice looking mare with a blaze face and white stockings. She was a little skittish and kept tossing her head and gazing off across the yard as though just having discovered something unusual. Queen was something else. She was a jugheaded, pot-bellied old harridan. She walked with her head down as if half asleep, but she knew what was going on every minute and was ready to make life difficult for me. I guess she sensed that I was an inexperienced kid and would test me to the limit.

I led them by their halter shanks, following along behind Freiburg's and Ernie's teams, half a mile on a winding wagon trail through a stand of young poplars to the hay field, Betty dancing and snorting and Queen trying her best to walk all over me.

The hay fields stretched flat like a sea, the timothy rippling in the drying wind. Beyond them to the east lay a shallow lake, a product of melted snow and spring rain. It would be a hay field like the rest later on when it dried up. Now it was host to hundreds of waterfowl bobbing and dabbling on its satin surface.

Freiburg and Ernie had started haying yesterday. They had five or six acres cut and lying flat when the thunderstorm hit. Two mowers stood, their blades hidden in the standing grass where they had been left when it started to rain. At the edge of the field, two rakes waited.

"You can take that rake on the left," Freiburg said to me. "We'll windrow this morning. It's drying pretty fast. By this afternoon, we'll be able to bunch and start coiling."

"Ernie, you take the other rake for a while. I'm going to cut some more."

I had never driven a rake, but I knew how one operated. I swung Betty and Queen on either side of the tongue, backed them, slipped the end of the tongue through the neck-yoke and fastened the traces. They were intent on cropping mouthfuls of green grass and I had trouble getting their attention. My shouts of "hudup" and "cut that out" didn't have much authority. My voice was changing and what was intended as a bellow frequently came out as a bleat.

As soon as I climbed up on the seat, I realized I was going to have trouble staying on it; my legs were too short to reach the frame and brace myself. I would have to slide part way out, drive with one hand and hang on to the seat with the other. Hitting the trip pedal was going to be pretty chancy.

It took a while, but I got a workable rhythm going. My windrows, pretty ragged to begin with, began looking straighter. Freiburg didn't interfere, he let me work it out on my own. It was hard work; old Queen made sure it was. She made me drive her every step; she wasn't giving anything away.

The sky stayed clear as the sun climbed and it was hot. The sweat ran down from under my cloth cap, and the dust clung to my face. We stopped for a drink of water about mid-morning. The sun and the breeze were doing their work; the hay was becoming brittle. We would be bunching and coiling this afternoon.

I didn't own a watch and I had no idea what time it was, but my stomach told me it was lunch time. My pancakes had been gone for quite awhile.

Betty's ears came forward and she cranked her head around, staring at the trail where it joined the field. From the poplars a buggy emerged, drawn by a single chestnut horse and occupied by old Mister O'Donnel and Berthe. Freiburg stopped mowing and waved.

"Dinner time," he hollered.

Ernie and I unhitched our teams and tied them to the rake wheels where they could feed on the windrowed hay. Berthe had a blanket laid out and was lifting pots and baskets out of the buggy. Old Mister O'Donnel stayed put, sitting on the seat. I guess it was more effort to get his arthritic body to the ground and then back up again than it was worth. The chestnut, old John, a thirty-year-old trotting horse and a veteran of the racing circuit, had given a good enough account of himself to be retired to pasture. His only chores were to pull the lunch buggy and make an occasional evening trot over the country roads.

Out of the pots and kettles came meat and vegetables, still hot and dripping with gravy. I had never smelled anything so good. There were pickles, bread, a bucket of tea, and great slabs of raisin pie for dessert. I ate until I couldn't stuff down another bite.

While Berthe gathered up the remains and loaded them into the buggy, Freiburg, Ernie and I flopped back onto the hay and closed our eyes. The horses needed time to eat, and it would be a long afternoon. I didn't hear the buggy depart.

We were all pretty lethargic, Freiburg, Ernie, me and the horses, stomachs still full and drowsy in the heat. We watered the horses at the lake and hitched them back to the machines, all except Jigs and Tony. They got tethered in the shade.

"Ernie, you can start coiling," Freiburg said, "I'm going to keep cutting. It's drying fast."

"Paul, you start bunching. You know how to bunch, don't you?"

"I guess not," I said.

"I'll show you." He climbed onto my rake, swung Betty and Queen and started lengthwise down the windrow, rolling up the hay into a bunch, loading the teeth until they rose off the ground, and then hitting the trip pedal. As the lever came forward he jammed his foot on it and held it until the teeth came clear, then he let it go. He did a couple of bunches and pulled up. I climbed up. The first time, I wasn't ready for the weight of the lever and it almost threw me off the rake. I made small bunches, until I got used to it.

The afternoon wore away, hot and dusty. Neat coils dotted the field. Ernie didn't say much, but he was a hard worker.

My rake had seen better days. Most of its paint was gone and it had a rusted, weathered look. The tongue—twin booms of hardwood about three inches square that came together to a single piece up near the neck-yoke—was broken. One of the booms had a long diagonal crack, starting a few feet ahead of the frame, that someone had nailed a piece of board across as a splint, a temporary repair and not a very good one. Bunching put a lot of strain on it, and the nails were beginning to work loose. It was flexing more and more as the afternoon wound down. I flagged Freiburg. Jim and Duchess, glad of the respite, stood swishing their tails and relaxing as he walked over.

"I think we better fix the tongue. It's getting pretty loose," I said. "It's bending a lot when I turn at the end of the row, and I'm afraid it's going to break right off."

He looked at it.

"I don't have a hammer or any nails," he said, pushing it with his foot. "It should be all right until quitting time. Take it easy. We'll fix it in the morning."

"I don't know," I said. "I don't like it . . ." I climbed back up.

I made a half a dozen more bunches, and the nails started pulling right out. I stopped again and looked at it. It wasn't going to hold until quitting time; I knew it. I waved at Freiburg.

"Keep going," he hollered, "It's almost quitting time. Keep going. We'll fix it tomorrow."

More nails pulled out. What had been a crack was becoming a complete break, gaping open as I turned at the end of the windrows. The last nails finally let go, and there was a snap as the boom splintered. The front piece sagged. The rear piece, still attached to the frame, became a long spear. As all the strain came on the other boom, it broke straight across. The front end, now not attached to anything, fell out of the neck yoke into the hay. All control of the rake was suddenly gone.

"Whoa!" I hollered, a reflex exclamation and probably not the right thing to say. Because I was turning at the end of a row, the teeth weren't loaded. Had they been, the rake would have stopped when the horses did, but being empty it continued forward a few feet. The splintered tongue, a hardwood spear a good two feet long, caught Queen in the rear end, a few inches to the right of her tail. Her reaction was immediate; she let drive with both feet. Her big hooves clanged against the frame, tilting it up and slewing it around. The spear point swung over and got Betty in the flank. She let drive.

"Whoa! Whoa!" I yelled, hauling on the reins with one hand while trying to keep my seat on the gyrating rake with the other.

That spear kept swinging from side to side, digging into first one mare and then the other. They kept trying to kick it away, hammering the remains of the tongue and the frame with both feet and getting tangled in the traces. All I could see were two pairs of huge hooves flying up in front of my face. I was hollering "whoa" and tugging on the reins, but they weren't paying any attention to me. I was afraid of falling forward into that melee of hooves and broken wood and was hanging on for dear life.

Both horses were getting panicky. I could see it coming, but nothing I said or did had any effect. They wanted to be free of the tangle of wood and metal that was bedeviling them, and, instinctively, they tried to run away from it. They took off, still kicking sky high. I stayed with them for awhile, trying to hold them and hollering "whoa" at the top of my voice.

If that broken pole sticks in the ground, it's going to flip me and this rake right on top of the horses, I thought.

I glanced over at Freiburg. He was waving at me to get off

and yelling. I let go the reins and rolled backwards, down over the teeth. I hit the ground in a ball and bounced. I knew right away that I wasn't hurt.

I sat up and looked at my rapidly disappearing team. They were still kicking and going full out. The rake was beginning to come apart, shedding teeth and anything else that was loose. I could see things flying off. Finally something broke and they were free. The rake, what was left of it, followed for a moment then slewed to a stop, its wheels at odd angles.

The horses kept going in a blind panic, still kicking wildly, but now their heels weren't connecting with anything. How far they would have gone is hard to say, and it would have been better had they been allowed to run themselves out, but the fence at the end of the field got in the way. They hit it, going full tilt. I heard the barbed wire screech and twang, and I saw a post break off and several more lean. Then they stopped.

Freiburg came running over.

"Are you all right?" he asked, a worried look on his face.

"I'm OK," I said.

"You should have got off of there sooner. You could have got bad hurt."

"I was trying to stop them," I said, "but there was nothing I could do."

"Once horses start to run away, there's not much you can do except let them run," Freiburg said, shaking his head. "That's all you can do."

Ernie came slouching over, but before he had a chance to say anything, Freiburg waved him away.

"You go and watch my team, Ernie," Freiburg said. "They're pretty excited. You better unhitch them and tie them up. We don't want another runaway. We'll go and get those mares untangled and see how bad they're hurt."

I felt sick and shaken, not so much for me; I was all right, but for my team and the rake. What had just happened was a blow to my pride. My new-found status as a man was suddenly on shaky ground. The horses could be badly hurt, and the rake looked like a pile of junk. I started walking toward the team. Freiburg, walking beside me, looked sober. Suddenly, I didn't feel very tall.

The horses were tangled in barbed wire, and they were cut. There was blood on them—on their chests, necks and forelegs, and it was dripping on the ground. I had trouble looking at it, and I had a salty taste in my mouth. They were afraid to move, wall-eyed and snorting, their nostrils flaring. We talked to them, quietly.

"Hooa there, girls. Whoa now, just take it easy. We'll get you out of there. Whoa now." I hadn't cried for a long time, but right now, it wouldn't have taken all that much . . .

We singled them up and worked them, one at a time, out of the wire.

I held them while Freiburg went over them, running his hands down their legs and under their bellies. They flinched as he touched their bruised heels. The harness was broken, so I led them. They snorted and shied away from the rake, ready to run again as we passed it. I tied them to a tree in the shade beside Jigs and Tony at the edge of the field.

It was near enough to quitting time and we were all kind of shaken, so we called it a day. It would take awhile for the horses to settle down, and anyway my rake was a mess. We retraced its path, picking up teeth. The axles were bent and the wheels were askew. It would take a few days to get it repaired.

We led the horses through the poplars back to the barn, Betty and Queen in between the other teams. They were all on edge, lathered with the sweat of excitement. We tied them in their stalls and fed them. We would water them later; they were too hot now.

I washed some of the dust off myself at the horse trough and went to the house.

Supper was a dreary affair. Nobody wanted to say much. Old Mister O'Donnel knew something had happened: he could tell somehow. He kept probing until Freiburg told him. Then he had plenty to say, particularly, about town kids and Germans. He shook his cane at Freiburg and me and called us every thing he could think of—none of it being complimentary. The only one who got off scot free was Ernie. He just sat there eating and saying nothing.

We ate and got out as soon as we could.

We watered the horses and gave them more hay. The barbed-wire cuts on Betty and Queen had partially dried, but their bruised legs were beginning to stiffen up and they limped to the water trough. There was little we could do; nature would have to heal them.

Father and Mother drove out just before dark and stopped at the end of the lane. I walked out to meet them and told them what had happened. I asked them to drive out tomorrow. I probably wouldn't have a job by then. O'Donnel would likely fire me—he would for sure if he listened to his father—and I might need a lift back home.

"You're sure you didn't get hurt?" Mother was all concern. Whether I had a job or not was secondary.

"I'm OK," I said.

We talked for a while and they drove off, both looking worried.

I crawled into my blankets. Reaction had set in, and I was worn out. I fell asleep and dreamed of horses hooves flying in front of my face. I awoke in a sweat, fell asleep and dreamed the same dream again. By morning I was a bundle of nerves.

Freiburg moving around woke me. He went downstairs without saying anything. Ernie stirred and hauled himself out of bed, yawning. We pulled on our clothes and followed. Ernie went to milk, and I went to the barn. Freiburg wasn't around.

I had fed the horses and was forking manure out of the stalls when O'Donnel came into the barn. I had never seen him before, but I knew who he was right away; he looked like his father, except that he was tall. He had the same hooked nose. He had on a red shirt and bib overalls, the legs tucked into calf-high, laced, brown leather boots. He had a straw cowboy hat, the same as his father's, shoved on the back of his head. He was smoking a cork-tipped cigarette, gripping it with his teeth like a cigar.

"You're Jones's boy?"

I nodded.

"I'm Bill O'Donnel." He ran a hand over Betty's rump and down her hind leg, probing a little around the heel. She winced and moved away. "What happened yesterday?" He had cold blue eyes, and he looked straight at me.

I told him, every last detail, trying not to lay blame on anyone. He nodded from time to time as I talked. He had an odd way of hunching his shoulders and rolling them around like a prize fighter. He kept moving as I described what had happened, but never took his eyes off me.

"Well, this team isn't going to be able to work, not for quite a while," he said as I finished, "and it's going to be at least a week before I can get the rake fixed."

I nodded. I wanted to say something to let him know that I would do just about anything to help repair the damage I felt I had caused.

"I'm sorry," I said. It was all I could think of to say.

"Freiburg," he said, shaking his head. "I should have known better . . . "

He walked into the stall beside Betty and looked at her chest.

"After breakfast, you get a pail of warm water and bathe both of these mares, I'll give you some Lysol to put in it. Now you better go and eat."

I passed Freiburg in the door as I left. As I started to wash at the horse trough, I heard him and O'Donnel talking inside the barn. Their voices got louder until they were shouting. I stood there, water dripping off me, listening. I couldn't hear what they were saying but they both sounded mad. I guessed it was my fault. I thought about getting my suitcase and blankets and walking away, but just then Freiburg came out.

He walked past me without saying anything and headed for the bunkhouse. In a few moments he came out. He had his suitcase and his blankets rolled loosely under his arm. He walked off down the lane to the main road, not looking back.

Ernie came from the corral with two pails of milk. He stopped beside me.

"Freiburg, he's gone, eh?"

"I guess so," I said.

I stayed on. It took awhile, but Betty's and Queen's wounds healed, and I drove them again. The rake got fixed, and we finished the haying, O'Donnel, Ernie and me. Great stacks, like big brown loaves, dotted the fields. And then there was the harvest: acres of wheat and oats to cut and stook. There was grain to haul and shovel when the threshing machine came.

We worked seven days a week, except that sometimes on a Sunday afternoon the Catholic priest would drive up, and O'Donnel would tell us to take the rest of the day off. He would disappear into the house and reappear only when the priest left. On those afternoons, Ernie and I harnessed old John to the buggy and went for a trot, just for a change of scenery.

I moved into the double bed with Ernie—on the side vacated by Freiburg—as the days became shorter and the nights colder. I got used to the dirt. In fact, one day I looked at my underwear and saw, without it bothering me too much, that it was the same colour as Ernie's.

My wages? Oh yeah. Thirty dollars a month and board . . . and I got to sleep in the bunkhouse.

13 • Walking Cold

IT WAS AFTER TEN WHEN THE KNOCK CAME ON OUR FRONT DOOR—A loud, startling sound in the quiet house. I was in bed just dozing off and came wide awake. Father stirred in the living room. I heard his newspaper slither to the floor and his grunt as he heaved himself out of his rocking chair.

"Who the . . . ?" he said. His vacated chair continued to rock on the rough board floor as he scuffed his way to the door.

"Who in the world is that?" Mother's voice came from the bedroom.

It was a rare event: somebody knocking on our front door. Even in the daytime it was unusual. Most people came to our kitchen door. There weren't that many who came, but those who did made stamping noises knocking the snow from their boots on the porch. Sounds that gave ample warning that somebody was there, somebody who expected to be invited in and wouldn't come in with snow on their boots. On a night when it was thirty below and after ten o'clock, a knock on the front door meant that whoever was there was somebody who didn't usually come to our house, somebody who didn't know that our front door wasn't the door to come to and who must have a pretty good reason for being there at all, at that time of night.

I slid out of bed and eased into the living room, far enough to see into the entry but back far enough that I wouldn't be seen standing there in my underwear. Father kicked the old blanket away from the crack at the bottom of the door and opened it. The ice seal broke with a crackle and there was a sucking sound as the tightly fitting door that hadn't been open for weeks was drawn inward. A tall man stood, filling the opening, frost on his coat and beard glistening white in the weak light spilling into the entry from the lamp in the living room. His breath and the vapour from inside the house billowed around him.

"I hope you weren't in bed, Jack, but I saw your light so I thought I'd stop." His voice, one I didn't recognize, was low pitched, and I had difficulty hearing what he said.

"Hewitt! What are you doing out this time of night? Come on in, man. Come in," I heard father say, a hearty ring to his voice.

He moved inside, filling the front entry with his bulk. Father closed the door. I still couldn't see who it was, but the name Hewitt was familiar. The rime-encrusted collar of his sheepskin coat was turned up, revealing no more than a wedge of his face, and his cap was pulled down on his forehead.

"I can only stay for a minute. It's about the boy. I can use him."

"Well, take off your coat and get warmed up. Can I make you a cup of tea? The wife's in bed, but I'll wake my daughter, she'll put the kettle on."

"No, no, I don't want to disturb you. I know you're going to bed. It's just that I wanted to let you know I can use the boy for a few weeks, probably until breakup."

"He's asleep, but I'll wake him." said Father.

"No, don't do that, but if he wants to work, get him to Miller's place before noon tomorrow. We'll be finished there in the morning and we'll be moving on up to Crocket's."

"Fine, Hewitt, I'll tell him. He'll be there. Now, are you sure I can't make you a cup of tea, something to eat . . . ? It's pretty cold out, something to warm you up. It won't take a minute."

"Thanks, no, Jack, I have to get going, get back to Miller's tonight, I'm driving back with Miller, but tell the boy . . . "

Now I knew who this man was who had come in the night and knocked on our front door: Hewitt Sides, a farmer from east of town—prosperous, people said, reason enough for Father to welcome him into our house, but someone whom Mother would have left standing on the doorstep. There was something about him, something sinister that people knew, but no one spoke of, a rumour of which I knew little and cared even less. I started forward, but then remembered I was in my underwear and stayed where I was.

He pulled the door open and stepped through the curtain of vapour into darkness.

"Good night, Jack, sorry to have disturbed you."

"Think nothing of it, thanks for coming by. I'll have him there in the morning. Good night, Hewitt."

A few fading steps squeaked in the snow, that was all, and then he was gone. Father kicked the blanket tight against the bottom of the door.

"Oh, you're awake," he said, seeing me standing beside the living room heater. "That was Hewitt Sides, he wants you to go to work on his baling crew. He wants you at Miller's before noon tomorrow."

"Baling crew? Miller doesn't have any hay. What's he baling?" I asked.

"Straw. He's baling straw, any kind of straw. They say the Saskatchewan government is buying straw, paying four dollars a ton for it. What with the drought, they don't have any hay, so they're buying straw." He shook his head in disbelief. "They don't have any straw, or hay, or anything else, for that matter, in Saskatchewan, that godforsaken province . . . dried right out. He wants you on his baling crew. Four dollars a ton for straw. That's good, better than burning it up in the spring."

"He wants me to shovel straw until breakup?"

"I guess so. Its pretty cold, but he's still baling. You'll be going. It's a job, you know."

"Yeah, I suppose so." I knew I didn't have much choice. "How did he know about me?"

"I met him last week. We were talking, and I mentioned that you could use a job."

"Did he say how much he's paying?"

"I think he said a dollar and a quarter a day and board. Not bad for shoveling straw."

"I guess its worth going for . . . a dollar and a quarter for shoveling straw . . . I guess I can be to Miller's before noon. I'll have to walk, I suppose. I'll start early."

"He said he's moving to Crocket's by afternoon, so if you're late, he won't be there."

"I'll be there." I said.

I went back to bed. I crawled in quietly against the warmth of my young brother who slept like a log and hadn't heard a thing. I lay listening to the house groan and creak, the unpainted shiplap, two-ply with tarpaper between, protesting in the cold. Father took the lamp into the bedroom, and I heard Mother and him talking. Then it was quiet, except for the creaking of the house and the low mutter of the fires. I lay in the darkness, watching the light devils winking through the warped lids of the kitchen stove and dancing on the ceiling, and I thought about working on a baling crew and tomorrow's walk in the cold. It was a cold that had hung over western Alberta for weeks, sunshine bright enough to sear the eyes, but no heat in it. Tomorrow I would walk in the sunshine and the cold and then I would shovel straw into a baling machine—I had no choice.

The darkness was still complete when I awoke. I could no longer hear the fire in the heater, and there was no sign of life from the cold black bulk that was the kitchen stove. There was a dead feeling in the room, this room that was the kitchen and was also where my brother and I now slept. Our bed, two cots, their legs interlocked, was in the corner. During the day they slid inside each other and became a couch covered with a checked throw rug. It was more than just a kitchen and our bedroom, this room. It was where we lived most of the time, where meals were cooked and eaten at the long oilcloth-covered table. Washing was done and hung to dry on lines strung above the stove, and snow was melted for wash water in a galvanized tank beside the stove. The stove was the core around which everything revolved, the centre of life in the rough board house that was our home through the short cold days and long cold nights of Alberta winters. By contrast, cooking on it—even just boiling the kettle—during the hot, mosquito-infested days of summer made the interior of the house unbearable.

I got out of bed and tiptoed across the ice-cold boards. I felt for a match on the shelf above the stove and struck it. Its flare hurt my eyes and I squinted at the clock on the cupboard; its hands stood at seven-twenty. It was early to be up. I usually slept solid until Father's grumbling around, shaking grates and banging stove lids, woke me. He was usually in a bad mood first thing in the morning, the result of having to get up and make fires, a job he felt my sister or I should be doing. I guess my mental alarm clock had sounded, warning me that today I needed to be up and moving earlier than usual.

I lit the coal-oil lamp on the table. By its yellow light I found paper and kindling, jammed it into the stone cold fire-box, and lit it. I filled the teakettle at the water-pail; a skimmer of ice had formed on it. The thin shiplap and tarpaper shell had given up its warmth to the February night, within minutes of the fire going out. I added more wood and crawled back into bed. My feet were numb.

I made tea in the big brown teapot, strong black tea, and I made porridge from rolled oats, letting it cook until it was almost solid and came out of the pot in chunks. I poured two cups of tea, added sugar and milk and carried them into the bedroom to Mother and Father.

I was at the kitchen table eating porridge with brown sugar and cream, the thick sweet liquid sending hot stabs of pain up through my cavities, when Mother came from the bedroom carrying the teacups. She put them on the cupboard and moved to the stove to stand in front of the open oven door. She stood there in her threadbare pink robe and her slippers that were rundown on the sides; a sick woman who looked old at fifty. Overweight and defeated, she spent most of her days in bed, delegating the cooking and washing to my sister.

"Make sure your insoles are dry," she said, taking them from the top of the warming oven and feeling them. "There are clean socks, and you had better take an extra pair of woollen mitts with you."

"I don't want to carry a lot of stuff," I said. "I'll be all right."

"You can't just go away, for maybe a month, without some extra clothes. What about some clean underwear and a shirt?"

"Gee whiz! Ma," I said, "I'm not going to carry a suitcase with me. I'll be OK."

"You had better make yourself a sandwich."

"I don't need to. I'll eat when I get to Millers.' They're going to feed me, you know. I'll be there before noon."

"I hate to see you go away with just the clothes you have on and only a bowl of porridge in your stomach. How cold is it; did you look at the thermometer?"

"I didn't look," I said, "but it's still cold, I know that."

Father came out of the bedroom and rattled around in the living room, putting wood in the heater and then came into kitchen.

"Why didn't you fix up the fire in the heater?" he growled.

He opened the kitchen door and looked at the thermometer on the post.

"It's about twenty-five below. It's warmed up a bit," he said, closing the door, "but you had still better watch out for frostbite."

"I'll be OK," I said.

"You don't have to go, you know." Mother said. "It's not

that much of a job, that baling. It's not worth freezing yourself for. If you had only stayed in school, you wouldn't have
to work outside in the cold. You could get an inside job, in a
bank or an office. You wait, I'll bet the Merryweather boys
don't go working on baling crews. They'll both get good jobs
inside, in offices. You wait and see. Why do you need to go
and work for that dreadful man, Sides? There's no future in
it, you know. Just always hard work out in the cold."

"Let him alone," said Father from his chair at the end of
the table where he usually sat, waiting impatiently for someone to cook his breakfast. "Work never hurt anybody.
Anybody who is anybody got there by working. If it wasn't for
his political connections, Merryweather and his boys might be
glad to be shoveling straw. Let him alone."

Mother carried the teapot and cups to the table.

"He's not going to make very much money at a dollar and
a quarter a day."

"It's better than what he's doing, sitting around reading
and going to that damned hockey rink. He's not making much
at that either."

"I guess I'll be going," I said. The argument had started
and I didn't want to be around to listen to it.

"Where are you going?" said my brother, sitting up in bed
and watching me lace up my boots.

"Millers.'" I said. "I won't be back, so you can have the bed
to yourself."

"Are you going for good. Do you mean it?"

"No, he's not going for good," said Mother, "just for
awhile, to work on a baling crew. You had better get yourself
out of that bed, too. Go and wake your sister."

"Before you go, you had better fill the wood box and get a
pail of water," said Father.

"I'd better get going if I'm going to be at Millers' before
noon," I said. It was a forlorn hope that just this once Father
might lower himself and go for a pail of water or bring in an
armful of wood.

"The chores have to be done, so you had better get at them." he said. I knew it was no use arguing.

I filled the wood box. I took the water pail along the path past the school to the town well. I had to break ice in the tank to get a bucket of water. The fire in the well house had gone out, so I lit it. If the pump froze it would crack, and nobody would get any water. I looked at the school on the way back. I wouldn't go there any more—not a chance.

"What's the point of an education? There aren't any jobs for educated people," Father had said last spring. He had got me a job haying, taken me out of school early to work on a farm. That job had ended with the harvest. "Work, that's what's important," he'd said. He really thought so, that is for everybody but him. He didn't work, not that he wasn't capable of work, but he had a pension from the war for some unspecified illness. Whatever it was, it didn't seem to incapacitate him from doing what he wanted to do, so that is what we lived on and he didn't work. He had an office from which he sold insurance, but few people had money to insure anything, so he spent his days talking politics in the barber shop or the beer parlour. He was also a Notary and a Justice of the Peace; jobs he had few qualifications for, but through some political machination, he had managed to become installed in them. Neither job paid more than a pittance. The wages I had earned last summer, haying and harvesting he had taken, leaving me just enough to buy winter clothing.

"Everybody has to pay their way. You might as well learn that right now." he'd said when I suggested that because I had worked for it for the whole summer, I should be allowed to keep at least part of it. He said it as if it was the best advice he would ever give me, the wisdom of the ages passed down from father to son. I had learned, all right. I had also learned that I wouldn't be going back to school, not ever—education, that was for other people.

The sun was up and shining through the haze that hung over town when I started out, heading west to Millers'.

Blue-grey columns from newly kindled fires rose above snow covered roofs: smoke trees blossoming white on top, not a breath of wind swaying their trunks. The tang of burning poplar hung in the air. Somewhere, someone was splitting firewood, the solid "chunk" of the axe hitting frozen wood came echoing across the skating rink. It was the only sound, other than the squeak of my rubber boots biting into the snow.

Down the hill past the blacksmith's shop and Hansen's barn, the road ran straight, polished by sleigh runners and speckled with frozen horse manure. I walked in the middle, kicking horse buns. We always kicked horse buns when we walked, anybody my age did. I laboured in the crackling air, breathing through my mouth to avoid freezing my nose, my exhalations puffing out in front of me and whitening the shawl collar of my sweater. There was no warmth in the sun on my back, but I was warm enough inside my layers of wool and denim. The exposed part of my face felt tight and the lobes of my ears tingled. I pulled my cap down.

At the fairgrounds, bits of faded ribbon and bunting still hung on the stock pens, a colourful reminder of the crowds and excitement of last September. Snow drifted against the door of the community hall gave it an abandoned look; it would take a long time to heat its frigid, echoing emptiness for a dance.

Squeak, swish, squeak, swish. The monotonous sound of my boots on the hard packed snow and the brushing of my denim coat sleeves against my body were all I could hear. I squinted in the strong light reflecting from the ice crusted snow.

A half mile beyond the fairgrounds, the land gave way, dropping down in steps to the river. The road, little more than a track, switch-backed from bench to bench. From the top, I could see across the valley to the squat grey buildings of Fred Teer's farm huddled at the base of the hill and his patchwork of fields rising above.

I walked briskly, down through the narrow traverses under

the hanging embankments which were riddled with the nest holes of swallows, out across the flats and through stands of dwarf poplars. Mine was the only shadow moving across the narrow frozen steppes. It was a winter road, used only when the river ice was strong enough to support horses and sleighs. To cross by the downstream bridge added a few more miles to get to the same place, the corner of Teers' homestead. I ran down the last steep pitch and out on to the iron hard surface of the river. Here, the bank was churned by hooves and littered with round water-washed stones, the bones of the river bank. They were uncovered as teams scrambled for a footing, their shoes digging through the thin covering of snow, as they strained to draw sleighs up off the ice.

Upstream was the black web of the railroad bridge spanning the valley, its shadow faithfully tracing each column and arch on the white expanse below. Close in on the far shore under the smoke grey smudge of willows, a coyote ghosted along searching out mice or snow-covered carrion, anything to sustain life. It was a hungry time for coyotes, a prolonged cold spell.

Should I stop at Teers' and stand beside their stove for awhile? I had better not; I still had a few miles to go, and I had no idea of time. Pauline would be there, though. My age and out of school to help on the farm, she and I had been friends as long as I could remember.

Up off the river I climbed, scrambling in the loose snow and gravel through the willow fringe to the main road. Across the way was the lane leading to Teers' house. I wondered what time it was. It was hard to tell by the sun; it didn't gain much height in February, and it wouldn't until the end of March. I would stop in and ask Pauline. She would know the time.

Teer was not a prosperous farmer. His stony ground couldn't produce hay and his grain crops struggled, barely growing high enough to cut. He wouldn't have straw to sell to the Saskatchewan government. His straw stacks, a hundred yards from the house, were being consumed by his few head of cattle that stood, hump-backed in the cold, trying to convert the thin nourishment into warmth.

Although there was no snow clinging to my boots, I stamped my feet on the porch at the kitchen door and knocked. Mrs. Teer, a tall, grey-haired woman, opened the door.

"Hello, Mrs. Teer," I said. She looked surprised.

"Paul! What are you doing here? Come in, Boy, don't stand there. Are you alone? Are you walking?" She looked past me as though expecting to see someone else. I stepped inside and closed the door.

"Yeah, I'm walking. I'm going to work for Sides. He's baling straw at Millers'. I'm supposed to be there before noon, but I didn't know what time it was, so I thought I would stop in and find out."

We both glanced at the clock hanging against the wallpaper, between the window and the stove. It was a china plate decorated with a Dutch scene painted in blue and with black numbers around the outside. A short brass pendulum hurried back and forth in a frantic effort to keep time. The hands stood at nine-thirty.

"It's nine-thirty if the train was on time. We set it yesterday morning by the train whistle. You know what train time is like, but it's about nine-thirty. Take off your coat, there's coffee in the pot. Pauline," she called, "come and see who's here."

Pauline, dressed to go outside, came into the kitchen. Her clothing was much like mine, a wool shawl-collar sweater under a denim jacket, denim bib overalls and rubber boots. A red wool toque covered her head, just wisps of her straight blonde hair stuck out from under it, that and her snub nose and smiling blue eyes.

"Hi," she said, "what are you doing here?"

I told her as I poured myself a cup of coffee. She came and stood beside me in front of the stove, extending her hands over the heat. I sipped on my coffee as my cap and mitts thawed in the warming oven.

"How's your mother and father?" Mrs. Teer asked from the sink where she was washing dishes.

"Fine," I said, not elaborating. She knew anyway.

We didn't have a lot to talk about, Pauline and I. We had talked about the things we would do when we were younger, but not now. Pauline had always wanted to be a nurse, but the chances of ever becoming one were slim. The best she could hope for was to marry into something better than she had, maybe a farm more productive than the barren acres on which her family now struggled. We stood there soaking up heat, hoping to take a little of it with us when we went back outside. Lately I had begun to see her as more than the child I had known most of my life. Whether one or both of us was changing, I hadn't worked out. But I knew I felt different when I looked at her.

"I had better be going," I said, though reluctant to leave the warmth of the kitchen and the companionable nearness of Pauline. "Thanks for coffee, Mrs. Teer."

"Goodbye, Paul, be careful your ears don't freeze. Pull your cap down, they're sticking out."

"Thanks, I will." I pulled the fur earflaps further down.

Pauline walked with me to the end of the lane.

"Will you make any money, baling?"

"Not a whole lot. It depends how long I work. Sides said until breakup—maybe a month."

"What will you do then, for the summer?"

"I don't know. I might work for Percy McLeod, if he's building anything. I'll probably go haying again. How about you?"

"I'll be here I guess. They need me. Dad is talking about going back to Ontario. I don't know. He's getting old. Maybe we would be better off there. I don't know."

We stood for a moment on the main road.

"Well, I guess I'll see you later." I said, "after the breakup. Bye . . ."

"Bye . . . don't freeze your ears, pull your cap down."

"Yeah, I will. Bye . . ."

I headed west, climbing up the benches out of the river valley to the country above, west to Millers', kicking frozen horse buns along the road. I wondered what time it was.

The road, straight as an arrow but undulating up and down, was bordered on the right by fences and on the left by the telephone line, its copper wire singing in the cold. My boots squeaked, and my sleeves swished against my body. I thought about Pauline moving to Ontario. All I knew about Ontario was its shape on the map, that it was on the Great Lakes and that Ottawa, the country's capital, was there. I couldn't imagine myself going to Ontario; in fact, I couldn't imagine myself being anywhere other than where I was. I had no driving ambition to go anywhere or be anything. A job, to earn money, was what I wanted. Not a lot of money—just some money, any amount to have in my pocket—money that was mine, that I could spend on a bottle of pop or pie and coffee down at Jim Mah's cafe if I felt like it. That's all I wanted. I swung my arms; my fingers in my leather mitts with their home-knit wool liners were going numb.

For the last while, I had been walking beside the yellow desiccated stubble sticking out of the snow on Miller's grain fields. Across on the far side, huddled together and leaning against a stand of poplars, stood his granaries. Where the snow-covered domes of their accompanying straw stacks should have been, blown there by the threshing machine, was a neat rectangular pile of bales, bales that I knew had been pounded out of Sides' baler. Of the baler or Sides, there was no sign, just the trampled snow and stubble, flattened where he and his machines had worked. A thin line of tracks made by the tractor and sleighs led toward the cluster of buildings at the top of a knoll a quarter of a mile ahead.

He's probably at the house waiting for me, I thought. It can't be noon yet. I walked faster, swinging my arms. My feet were cold, the front of my coat was covered with frost, and I was hungry. I would be glad to get to Millers', stand beside a stove and eat something.

Miller was in the yard, hitching a team of horses to a sleigh. He was fiddling with one of the traces as I approached. He had his back to me and jumped, startled, when I spoke.

"Hello Mr. Miller," I said.

A short stocky individual, he was bundled in sheepskin, making him look rather like an Eskimo. His face took on a sour expression when he saw who it was. He was unshaven and his nose was running, the drip forming an icicle on his tattered moustache. A misshapen home-rolled cigarette smouldered in the corner of his mouth. A nervous man, his movements as he worked around his horses, were jerky, making them fidget.

"If you're Jones's boy, you're too late; Sides is gone," he said, clipping his words as though begrudging having to squander them on me.

"Too late! What time is it. How long has he been gone?" I asked, dismay making my voice go up and the questions sound desperate.

"What difference does it make? He's gone. Said to tell you he's gone to Crockets'. Couldn't wait."

"But he said he wouldn't go until noon. When did he leave?"

"Couldn't wait for you. You should have been here earlier. He's gone to Crockets', about an hour ago. You might be able to catch him, if you don't stand around here talking."

"I'm pretty cold," I said.

"It's cold out, that's why," he said as he climbed into his sleigh. "Heah . . . gidap," he hollered at his team. He drove off without looking back.

I stood there at a loss, looking at Miller's retreating back hunched over on the seat, plumes of steam from the nostrils of his trotting horses puffing out on either side of him. I was cold, hungry and didn't quite know what to do.

Millers' squat log house looked inviting with its thread of smoke standing above its rusted stovepipe. I was torn between knocking on the door and asking Mrs. Miller to let me get warm and maybe give me something to eat or continue on, cold as I was, and hurry after Sides. The longer I waited, the further away Sides would get. I turned toward the road. West I went, walking fast, following the lug marks of the tractor wheels punched into the hard-packed surface of the road. Squeak, swish, squeak, swish. The sun on my left was as high as it was going to get and starting to swing around in front of me. It must be noon or after, but it didn't matter what time it was now. Sides was gone. If I had to walk all the way to Crockets', I still had as far to go, or farther, than I had already come. The road undulated ahead, bars of shadow from the telephone poles lying across it. I pulled my cap down over my ears and walked as fast as I could, pounding my hands against my sides to keep the circulation going.

I squinted into the distance, hoping to see movement ahead, the moving machinery that would be Sides' outfit. At the end of Miller's land, the tractor marks turned right at the junction, heading north. I followed. A mile north at the next junction they turned west again through muskeg. The tall black needle-pointed spruce cast sawtooth shadows at an angle across the road.

The exertion was keeping me warm except for my feet encased in rubber boots. The perspiration, unable to get out, was wicking heat away, and I had long since given up any sensation in my toes. The sun, weak as it was, was keeping my face from freezing, but a thick layer of frost had formed on my wool collar and the front of my coat. I had no other option but to keep moving.

From the top of a knoll, I saw it, a glint, perhaps from a window in the bunk car. Then as I hurried forward, the bulk of the machinery with figures moving around came in sight. They were stopped on the side of the road. I caught up. Sides and his son Wilton were tinkering with the tractor from which black smoke was issuing. Three other figures were standing looking on. I knew them all: Johnny Semenuik, Johnny Laschuck and

Dave Dorsawich. All were stamping their feet and swinging their arms to keep warm. Their coats and hats, like mine, were covered with frost. Like me, they had all been walking.

"Hello, Johnny," said Sides, looking up from peering at the tractor. "I thought you weren't coming. We couldn't wait any longer, not without the tractor freezing up. I thought you'd be along earlier, if you were coming. Did your dad drive you to Millers'?"

"No, I had to walk, our car is up on blocks for the winter. I missed you by about an hour. I'm glad you stopped or I wouldn't have been able to catch up."

"That's a pretty good hike you've had. Well, it's only another few miles to Crockets'. We're all walking. If Wilton can get this carburetor adjusted we'll get moving again. Do you know everybody?"

"Yeah."

"This is Jack Jones's boy," he said, addressing the others.

They all nodded at me, looking me up and down, trying to decide whether I was going to be a help or a hindrance on the straw stack.

"Hey! you're growing up, almost as big as a man," said Dorsawich. The Russian-accented words come slowly out of a grey mass of frost-encrusted beard. "You were just a little kid when I saw you last, hey . . ." He shook his head in disbelief, "and here you are, working. Well, I hope you can work fast enough to keep warm, hey . . ."

The tractor noise increased and the smoke abated. Wilton climbed up on the seat, engaged the clutch and with a jerk the train of machinery—tractor, bunk car, equipment sleigh, and baling machine—moved forward in a long column. The tractor snorted and bounced along on its big lugged wheels; the rest squeaked and groaned in the cold. The sun was dropping rapidly toward the western horizon. I walked behind with the others, but now there was more than the squeak of my boots and swish of my own clothing keeping me company. There was someone to talk to although it was an effort to talk and walk in the cold, and we didn't have a lot to talk about. The others had been together most of the winter and were talked out. I was the kid and discounted as having anything of any consequence to say. So we walked behind the train saying little. The two Johnnys, when they spoke, did so in Ukrainian and only to each other. Dave Dorsawich strode along in silence, a huge curved-stemmed pipe clamped in his teeth, and me—my feet two unfeeling lumps, my stomach scraping my backbone and the cold seeping through to my bones— bringing up the rear. I just wished we would get there, anywhere to get warm. Hewitt Sides rode the tractor with Wilton.

There wasn't much light left when Crockets' big barn loomed ahead. Wilton turned the tractor through a wire gate into a field and headed straight across, breaking trail through the thin coverlet of snow over a ploughed field to a couple of big straw stacks. Glad of a change from the boredom of walking, we jumped to the task of uncoupling the train of machinery and hitching the individual units to the tractor for positioning, the bunk car to one side, the baler next to the stacks and the equipment sleigh in between.

The bunk car was barely in place when Johnny Semenuik, who was the cook, disappeared inside to get a fire going in the stove and get a pot of coffee on. Dave, Johnny Laschuck, and I took a couple of axes and walked to a fringe of willows to cut firewood. We dragged a tangle of dry limbs and built up a pile under the now silent tractor. In the morning, it would be sprinkled with gasoline and ignited. By the time the wood was consumed, the under parts would be warm and the oil thin enough to hand crank it—an impossible job without heat. Wilton was draining the radiator into a bucket and was wreathed in a cloud of steam.

One end of the bunk car contained bunks filled with straw, two singles, one above the other, on the left and two doubles, one above the other, on the right. The two Johnnys slept in the lower double. I would sleep with Dave in the upper double, while Wilton and Hewitt slept in the singles. At the end near the door was a table with benches at the sides and a chair at one end, a cook stove, and a series of apple boxes stacked and nailed to the wall, serving as cupboards. Above the stove was a clothesline: a place to dry mitts, insoles and socks. The only light came from one small window and a bracket wall lamp above the table. The pungent smell of unwashed socks, sweaty clothing and fried food hit me as I entered, but it was warm and there was coffee bubbling and food being cooked in big frying pans—steak, fried potatoes, and beans—in big quantities.

I ate as I thawed out, not letting the throbbing of my feet deter me from the business at hand.

"It's funny," said Hewitt, from his place at the end of the table, "here we've got six guys, and three of them are named Johnny: Johnny Semenuik, Johnny Laschuck and now Johnny Jones. That's funny, three out of six guys named Johnny." He chewed thoughtfully as though having discovered something that would change the rotation of the earth.

"My name isn't Johnny," I said. "It's Paul."

He stopped chewing and laid down his knife and fork. He leaned toward me, looked straight into my face, started chewing again and then swallowed.

"Paul, is it?"

I nodded.

"Well, Johnny, that does come as a surprise. Do you hear that, eh!" he said looking at the others and shaking his head. "Never mind Johnny, It doesn't matter." He went on eating. No one said anything; they were too busy with steak and potatoes.

I was Johnny. I don't think I could ever have convinced them otherwise. I never mentioned my name again.

It wasn't late, but I almost fell asleep at the table. There was no dallying over coffee; everybody headed for the bunks. It was either that or sit on a hard bench at the table. Johnny Semenuik had dishes to do and preparations to make for breakfast. Nobody offered to help.

I awoke some time in the night. The lamp was still burning. My face was inches away from the massive grey tangle that was Dave Dorsawich's beard, and I was being bathed in his ripe, pipe-smoke tainted breath. I turned over, glancing down into the kitchen area as I did so. Johnny Semenuik was sawing on a piece of boxwood. On the table was a picture frame he was making from tiny triangles sawn from the sides of apple boxes and glued together. He worked on it in the night and slept between preparing meals in the daytime. I went back to sleep, wrapped in a blanket that had seen a winter's use without the benefit of a wash or an airing. The straw had worked itself into lumps and bare patches and the boards underneath were hard, but I slept.

When next I awoke it was morning, but it was still black outside and the lamp was still lit. Wilton came in. He had started the fire under the tractor and the flames played on the window. Johnny Semenuik had huge piles of pancakes on the table and a big enamel coffee pot sat steaming on the stove. There was nowhere to wash; we just moved to the table, half dressed, and began eating as though just continuing where we left off last night.

There would be no baling without the tractor. If it started, we worked; if it didn't, we had nothing to do. Hewitt, on the seat, adjusted things as Wilton turned the crank. Nothing happened. He turned some more, straining to move it faster. He let go, puffing. Johnny Laschuck grabbed it. A big strapping man, he got it spinning faster. A little puff of smoke issued from the exhaust pipe.

"A little more and you got her," said Dorsawich, standing back and looking wise, his pipe in his hand.

Johnny let go, massaging his arm and mouthing Ukrainian epithets.

"Here, Johnny," he said to me, "twist her tail, sonomabitch."

I grabbed the crank. I could hardly move it, but I was not about to give in easily with everybody watching. I threw my full weight on it and by using every ounce of strength, I turned it over and kept it going through one, two, three revolutions. There was a bang as it fired, "You got it, Johnny, give her a little more." I kept turning, almost coming apart inside. It fired again and kept firing. Hewitt fiddled frantically with levers and it settled into a roar.

Johnny Laschuck slapped me on the shoulder.

"Hey, you sure can start tractors, mebbe you gonna be engineer, hey."

The day's work could begin. It was almost daylight and just as cold as yesterday.

We shovelled straw, handing it along one to the other. Hewitt, standing on a wooden platform, fed it into the baler where the ram pounded it into bales. Wilton threaded the wires through and tied them when the bale was big enough. As each one was nudged out by the succeeding one, he picked it up and stacked it. It was mindless work. The straw lay as it had been blown by the threshing machine; no pattern to it. There was no way to get a good forkful so we just shovelled it along, hour after hour. No one said anything. There was just the roar of the tractor and the pounding of the baler.

At noon we climbed down off the stack leaving the machinery running. We ate steak and potatoes washed down with coffee, sitting at the table in the bunk car. There was no talking—there was nothing to talk about that hadn't been said. We climbed back up on the stack and began shovelling again. Standing on straw rather than on hard packed snow, my feet didn't get as cold, and the exertion kept my body warm. Without that to think about, my mind wandered, skipping from one thing to another, going in circles. I had no conception of time.

There had been no wind for weeks, just the steady cold and sunshine. Some time—it must have been late afternoon—I noticed a milky haze creeping over the sky, and there was the odd puff of wind catching the straw and blowing it away. It began to feel warmer; the bite had gone out of the air. Dave Dorsawich pointed at the a pair of sun dogs bracketing the sun.

By the time Wilton shut the tractor off and we slid down off the stack, we had our coats unbuttoned.

"Chinook, by golly, she's coming," said Dave.

We cut more willows and stacked them under the tractor— just in case the Chinook petered out—and went to the bunk car. I sat there, bone weary, eating steak and potatoes. Johnny Semenuik was still washing dishes when I fell asleep. When I awoke, wind was buffeting the bunk car, rocking it on its sleigh, and the frost that had accumulated on the walls in the corners remote from the stove was melting and running down in rivulets.

The tractor started easily, and we were again shovelling straw by daylight. By mid-morning we were shedding coats and working in shirt sleeves. Hewitt began casting his eyes across the fields and looking concerned. The snow was disappearing and the ploughed earth was showing through. Water was lying in puddles around where we were working. The baler and the bunk car were mounted on sleighs as was the equipment trailer carrying baling wire and gasoline in barrels. Without snow, the tractor wouldn't be able to move them. Was this the breakup? It was early, but the likelihood of getting any amount of new snow was slim. The wind continued unabated.

By the following morning there was little snow left, just patches in the lee of the willows. Hewitt sat at the end of the table eating and looking morose.

"I guess we're going to have to call it off and head for home while there's still enough snow on the road," he said, looking at each of us in turn. "It's too bad, but I don't want to get stuck here."

"Mebbe it will snow more." Johnny Laschuck said.

"And maybe it won't," said Dave, puffing on his pipe and looking wise.

I didn't care that much if I didn't have to shovel any more straw. I liked the Chinook and the prospect of spring.

"So I guess we'll pack it up and head for home," said Hewitt.

We made up the train—the tractor, the bunk car, the baler, and the equipment sleigh—strung out in a line. The sleigh runners squeaked over the bare earth of the field to the road where the hardpacked snow had turned to ice. We walked behind on ice or in mud, saying little.

At the road junction, where Sides would head straight south to his farm and I would head east to home, the train halted.

"Well, Johnny, I guess I'll have to pay you off," said Hewitt, handing me two dollars and fifty cents. "It's too bad it couldn't have lasted a little longer, but that's how it goes sometimes."

"Thanks," I said, "maybe next year."

"Yeah, maybe next year. Goodbye, Johnny, say hello to your dad."

"Goodbye, Johnny," said Dave, "don't spend all that money in one place."

"He's gonna take his girl to the dance and then get drunk on all that money," said Johnny Laschuck, grinning. "Goodbye, Johnny."

The tractor snorted and the train squeaked and groaned forward.

I headed east, clumping along in my rubber boots, my coat slung over my shoulder and the fur flaps on my cap turned up.

14 • The Sellout

MY AWAKENING WAS A WARRING BETWEEN LUCIDITY AND TROUBLED dreams. Lucidity finally gained the upper hand, and with a start I became fully conscious. It would be the last time I would awake in this house. I lay with my nose poking out from under the covers, trying to decide how I felt about that and various other things that were about to change my life forever. It was early and the room was cold and quiet. There was nothing unusual about cold; it was always cold in the morning in our house. The fires invariably burned themselves out in the small hours. I thought about getting up and lighting them, a responsibility that Father had shifted on to me last year, but this morning I lay there putting it off. The cold had nothing to do with my disinclination to leave the quilts. It was because I knew that once I got up a whole train of events would be set in motion, and when the day had run its course everything would be gone, even the bed I was lying in.

Today we were selling out. This morning the contents of our house, garage, and yard would go on the block at a public auction to be sold for whatever could be pried from the pockets of those who would come to it—people from the town and surrounding farms—people with little money to spend.

By the thin March light seeping through the window, I could see the cardboard boxes under the table partially filled with the things we were keeping—a few dishes, knives and forks, a frying pan and a pot or two—all packed in layers of newspaper. Things we would need at the coast, that mythical place that beckoned from beyond the western mountains.

We never referred to it as British Columbia. Everyone around town who talked about it, it was just "the Coast." We were going there tomorrow. In the morning we would board the train for Edmonton where we would change for one going west to the Coast.

I had no mental picture of the Coast. All I knew was hearsay: that it was a place of big trees that, unbelievably, took sometimes as long as a day to chop down, where clouds hung below the mountain tops. The winters were mild, and somehow the Pacific Ocean was involved, washing against a rocky coastline, but I couldn't visualize it. Everybody seemed to think it was the promised land where there was work and wages for doing it. For the last year it was a poor month when at least two families hadn't pulled up stakes and left for Vancouver, prompted by rumours trickling back that so-and-so had got a job. Auction sales had become the norm. We were following the trend; our sale was scheduled to start at eleven o'clock.

I felt no excitement about going. I thought I should, but I didn't. I had no burning desire to go anywhere. There was no specific place that I wanted to be. On the other hand, I wasn't at all reluctant to leave this town where I had spent most of my teen years. Any pangs I did feel were offset by the thought of the dull grey lifestyle we had here. I would go anywhere if it meant things would be different, how different didn't matter. Different meant better.

I rolled over and stared at the ceiling. Above the stove, it was black with soot. Every time the lid was taken off to push more wood into the firebox, a little more soot was added. This room, lined with shiplap lumber, the nail heads tufted with frost, was the kitchen, crowded and reeking with trapped odours of cooking, heavy winter socks drying, rancid rubber boots and stale wood smoke. It was where my brother and I slept. I wouldn't be sorry to leave it.

The icy nails in the floor drilled into the bottoms of my feet as I stood up. I didn't own any slippers so I lifted my heavy socks from the clothesline that spanned the full length of the room and pulled them on.

I lit the fire for the last time, wondering as the kindling crackled and light winked through the cracks in the top (distorted by hundreds of too-hot fires) who would buy an old stove like this and for how much. I filled the kettle from the water bucket.

"Hey! Wake up," I said, shaking my brother. "We've got to get moving, have breakfast and carry all of this stuff outside. You better get up."

"I don't want to go to no coast. I'm staying," he grumbled into the pillow.

"You can stay if you want," I said, "but you better get up anyway, or we'll sell the bed with you in it."

"Stupid coast. I ain't going."

He was the only one of us dead set against going. He had been since it was first mentioned, but being the youngest he didn't have much choice. Even my sister Olwyn, who had a boy friend that she was reluctant to leave, had come around to thinking that there wasn't much future here and was willing to seize the opportunity for something better. But like me she had only an ill-defined idea of what we were going to. It wasn't as if we had been asked if we wanted to go; none of us had. Father had told us we were going, and that was that. I hadn't objected because I couldn't think of one good reason why I shouldn't go. I was, at seventeen, without definite thoughts about my future. I had no clearly defined goals. I had some vague thought about owning a truck with which to go into the hauling business, but the amount of money needed to acquire one was so vast as to be beyond the limit of imagination. So I was adrift on a sea of indifference. I could be led anywhere, and the Coast was as good as anywhere else.

Olwyn came out of her room, her dark hair tousled and her eyes heavy. She filled a pot with water and rolled oats, going through the motions automatically. Her mind, still clouded with sleep, wasn't functioning yet.

"Tea! . . ." Father's voice came grating from the bedroom.

It was an exceptional morning when this irritating demand didn't come rasping from the stuffy confines of the room where he and Mother slept. I was expected to make tea and carry a cup to his bedside, and woe betide me if the sugar and milk wasn't right. This morning, despite the fact that we were pressed for time, was no exception. He had to have his tea in the best English tradition, by his bed, first thing in the morning.

"His majesty calls," said my sister, rolling her eyes. "You had best get it in there, and we better get breakfast over or people will be coming to the sale and we won't be ready."

"Owen, get out of that bed and get your clothes on."

"Stinking coast," he said, finally dragging himself out from under the mound of bedding, but then sitting in his underwear in no hurry to dress.

"Tea! . . ." He would keep hollering until I delivered it. I hated that sound. I poured a cup, hoping it had brewed enough, added milk and sugar and carried it into bedroom. The fetid air in the small room, scarcely wider than the brown metal bed frame, struck me almost a physical blow. With little ventilation, the smell of unwashed bodies, bed clothes that had been used all winter without airing, stale cigarette butts from the overflowing ashtray, and the stink from the enamel pot under the bed were overpowering.

"What took you so damned long?" he growled as he heaved his way up in the bed and extended an unsteady hand for the cup I had set beside the coal-oil lamp on the upended orange crate that served as his night table. I didn't say anything. It was no use reminding him that it took awhile for ice-cold water to come to a boil. He scowled at me. In the dim light he looked like a thick, tousled bear. The grey chest hair escaping from the unbuttoned top of his Stanfield's underwear and the day-old growth on his face gave him an untidy, mossy look. He took a noisy slurp and then reached for his cigarette makings. He had come home late last night and there was still the smell of liquor on him.

On the other side of the bed, Mother didn't stir. She was facing the wall, a quiet mound under the quilts. She had been ill a long time. Her health was the reason we were moving— the reason we gave, anyway. There were other reasons, but we didn't talk about them. She would spend the day at the neighbours. She had no strength to do anything. She would be better out of the way. We would spend the night at the hotel or farmed out among people who were still our friends, and tomorrow take our leave.

I went back into the kitchen and stood by the stove. My sister was stirring the porridge pot. The steam from it and from the kettle was accumulating on the windows, adding to the paisley frost patterns already there. It was cold out, maybe ten below. Not a good day for an auction sale.

"Do you think anybody will come and buy anything?" she asked. "Suppose they don't, what are we going to do with it?"

"They'll come," I said. "Don't worry."

I could not imagine an auction sale to which nobody came; they always came, no matter what the weather. The thought of a bargain was irresistible. They would come, the farmers with manure on their boots, bundled in their sheepskins and mackinaws, wool caps with fur earflaps pulled down and overalls tucked in high rubbers, most with pinched unshaven faces and desperate eyes. They would paw through our stuff and then stand, puffing on their ragged home-rolled cigarettes as they offered as little as possible, trying to conceal their paltry bids behind an air of nonchalance. I had seen it happen at other sales. I had gone to a lot of them in the last year, not to buy anything but because they were free entertainment, something to go to when there was nothing else to break the monotony.

We wouldn't be rich at the end of today.

"I'm not going to school today," said Owen. "I'm going to help with the sale."

"You're going to school," said Father, emerging from the bedroom carrying his teacup. "It'll probably be the last day you'll ever go to school, so make the most of it. When we get to the Coast, you'll be going to work."

"I'm not going to the Coast. I'm staying."

"Don't talk nonsense. What do you think you're going to do here? Do you think anyone's going to take you in . . . let you live with them for nothing? Forget it. Now get yourself dressed."

Owen had a stubborn streak. He had his heels dug in and, although I knew he would eventually capitulate, he would argue the point as long as possible. He pulled on his pants and slid onto a chair behind the table, his jaw set and a look on his face that said push me hard enough and I really will stay. He was big for fifteen and strong. He could work and if he could find a job he could turn in a fair day—if he could find a job.

Olwyn ladled porridge into bowls.

"Go easy on the milk, that's all there is," she said.

"What's this? . . . porridge . . . you know I don't eat porridge." Father recoiled from the bowl. "Where's the toast?"

"There isn't any bread or butter or anything else. The cupboard is empty. All there is, is porridge," said Olwyn. "Sorry, but that's it. And we have to get the dishes washed and everything outside, and we don't have a lot of time to do it."

"I'll eat downtown. I'm not eating porridge."

"It wouldn't hurt you for one morning." Mother appeared from the bedroom bracing herself on the door frame as she moved unsteadily into the kitchen.

"I'm not eating porridge. I'll eat downtown. I've got some business to clean up anyway. I'll eat at Jim Mah's."

"What about the sale?" I asked. "We've got to get all of this stuff ready."

"Well. You don't have anything better to do. You and Olwyn can get it outside. It won't take long."

Somehow I had known that was the way it would be.

"I'll get dressed." Mother said. "Olwyn, will you help me? I know you're busy, but if you'll help me, I'll go over to Stickles'. They'll give me a cup of tea and some toast, I'm sure . . . I wish I was stronger. I'd like to stay and help but I know I'd just be in the way. Now, Paul, make sure everything is clean. I'd hate to have people making remarks. I remember when Fords sold out. The auctioneer made jokes about the dishes being dirty. I don't want that to happen to us."

Outside, it was cold and cloudy. Typical mid-March weather. The ground in the yard was icy. The Chinook had gone through a couple of days ago melting everything but the biggest drifts down to bare earth, and then it had turned cold again. At least it wouldn't be muddy underfoot as long as it stayed that way. I began dragging stuff off the porch out to the yard.

I struggled with our old washing machine. It was an awkward thing with its heavy wooden tub and big handle on top. I had spent many an hour working that big handle in the steam-filled kitchen on washday. Not an easy job with a load of heavy winter underwear and shirts in it. Mother had been proud of it when we brought it home, the smell of varnished wood still strong and the gold lettering still bright. Who would want it now, I wondered.

I carried our sleds and skis, our garden tools, the few carpenter's tools that had built our house, the axes and saws, their handles slicked by the palms of horsehide mitts showing the hour after hour Owen and I sawed and split poplar to feed our winter fires.

The notices that we had tacked on buildings and poles weeks ago had advertised the things we were selling: stoves, furniture, dishes and a lot of other stuff. Among it all, somehow, our old galvanized washtub got listed as a bathtub. Granted we used it to bathe in, had done since I could remember, but it wasn't a bathtub.

"I'm coming to your sale to bid on that bathtub," a couple

of people had said. I hadn't set them straight. Without that attraction, they might not come. I carried it out to the yard and set it beside the washing machine.

Mother came out, bundled in her coat, a scarf wrapped around her face and a wool toque pulled down over her hair. A short heavy woman, she had a heart condition that had kept her confined to the house most of the time.

"Will you walk with me over to Stickles', Paul? Olwyn is so busy. My . . . the air smells nice. I've been cooped up in the house for so long, I've forgotten what fresh air smells like."

"Maybe at the Coast you'll get out more," I said. "At least it won't be as cold. They say it will be spring when we get there, with leaves and grass and everything. It's hard to believe, though."

"You'll love the Coast," she said, a far away look in her eyes. "I can't wait to see the ocean again. Maybe I'll walk on a beach, like I did when I was a girl. If I can just get a little stronger . . . maybe the lower altitude . . . The doctor says it should be easier on me."

We walked across the road and through the vacant lot across the way, she leaning heavily on me, placing her over-shoe-clad feet carefully on the icy path. It was a narrow path through young trees, a shortcut that we used to go to school and the United church. I hung on, supporting her weight and pushing the bushes to one side. She was gasping as I helped her up the steps to Stickles' porch, and her legs were shaking.

"I'll be all right now," she said. "Just let me catch my breath for a moment. You go on back and get things ready. I just can't wait to get this sale over and get away. There's nothing here for us now. We'll all be so much better off at the Coast."

"You'll be all right now?"

"Yes, I'll be all right. You go ahead."

She rapped at the door.

"You're not selling my skis." Owen was in the yard with

them in his hand. He looked belligerent, daring me to disagree with him.

"What do you think you're going to do with those old skis, ski down Main Street in Vancouver?"

"I'm not going to Vancouver," he said, walking away, the skis dangling from his hands. He took them into the garage.

Olwyn was packing bedding into two trunks. Those and three boxes would be shipped. In them would be everything we owned. Not much to show for all the years we had lived here.

"You can start taking the beds apart," she said. "I've got the bedding packed."

"I'm going downtown now," Father said. He was dressed in his suit and he was putting on his grey fedora. He pulled it down over his eyes like the slouch hat worn by the Shadow, but on him it didn't quite come off. It didn't give him a sinister appearance. It sat on his bullet head like it didn't belong there.

"I'll need help getting some of these things outside," I said, "the kitchen cupboards and the beds. You know . . . the big stuff. I can't get them through the door by myself."

"What's the matter with you, are you some kind of a weakling? You should be able to move those few things. They're not heavy. Olwyn can give you a hand if you need one. I've got to go. Make sure Owen goes to school." He went out the door, up the road and over the brow of the hill without a backward glance.

"I'm sure the business he has to attend to is very important," said Olwyn, "like, maybe lifting a few with the boys? Anyway he's out from underfoot. Let's get on with it."

I looked around for Owen, but I didn't see him. I guessed he'd gone to school.

We got the big things out first and then set the small things on them. Out in the yard, in the cold light of day, it looked like what it was, a bunch of junk—homemade furniture that had never seen paint, chipped dishes, most having come as premiums out of Quaker Oats, sagging bed springs, a few worn scatter rugs, and a couple of rolls of Congoleum— nothing with any intrinsic value. I began to understand, a little, why Mother and Father didn't want to be around. Even I was a little shamed by its appearance.

The stoves would come out last after they had cooled down. Someone would give us a hand with them.

By ten-thirty most of it was out and arranged so that people could walk around and look at it. The auctioneer and his assistant drove up in his Buick sedan.

A big florid man with a midsection that extended well out over his belt, Art Knight had been an auctioneer for a lot of years. He was one of the few people in the country who had prospered from the general exodus. His talent for extracting the last few cents for every item on the block was legend, making him much in demand. This morning he was dressed in a brown three-piece suit, polished shoes, a homburg hat, and a chesterfield coat. Through the unbuttoned fronts of his coat and jacket, I could see a heavy gold watch chain glistening as it looped across his paunch. The smell of shaving lotion lingered after him as he moved between the heaped contents of our home. He was not enthused by the prospect of trying to sell it; that much was evident by his look of distaste. I guess he was mentally calculating what each item would bring and the likelihood of selling any of it for substantial sum seemed dismal. He moved things, lifted lids and peered inside, held the odd piece up to the light, his jowled face becoming more dour by the moment. This sale was not going to make him much richer.

"Where's your dad?" he finally asked.

"He went downtown," I said. "Do you need him?"

"No, I guess not, but I thought he would be around. You'll have to move this stuff as I call for it . . . hold it up so the bidders can see it. Do you think you can do that? Is this everything?"

"There's the kitchen stove and the airtight heater. They

were too hot to bring out. Maybe they're cool enough now, but I need a hand to get them outside. As soon as somebody comes, I'll get them to help me." He nodded and turned. He contemplated the yard and its contents. A deep rumbling rose from somewhere within him, vibrating his jowls as he stood there ruminating. He asked me to move a few things and bring something for him to stand on, a few boards, anything to keep his polished shoes up off the icy yard. He indicated where he would stand, a place where he would see every upraised finger and flicking eyelid that would indicate a bid. His assistant Tom, a thin clerical man with a pinched face and a runny nose, laid out his record book on a couple of stacked apple boxes and seated himself on a kitchen chair, his head pulled down inside the collar of his overcoat—his office was open. He wiped his nose and then sat with his hands in his pockets, waiting to record something.

They started coming, the rigs with farmers hunched on the seats, drawn by horses coated with frost from their own laboured breathing. Some were wheeled conveyances, but most were runnered still taking advantage of the scraps of snow and ice left on the roads. There were stout sleighs with grain boxes, light cutters, and sleds made from naturally curved tree trunks fastened with wooden pins and baling wire. There were a few Bennett buggies—those wondrous vehicles fashioned in a dozen different ways from automobile chassis, the engines discarded because of the lack of wherewithal to buy gas for them—sliding and bouncing around on their rubber-tired wheels. The horses were a rag-tag mixture, ranging in size from Shetland ponies to big cross-bred Belgians and Percherons. Few teams were matched for size or colour, all were wearing the shaggy coats of late winter.

These people were the settlers of the thirties, immigrants from central Europe who in the past ten years had pre-empted every last quarter section in the country. Most eked out a bare existence, and their faces showed it. They had furnished their rough log cottages and equipped their farms with things bought at auction sales like ours.

They pulled off the road in front, unhitched the horses and tied them to the sleigh-boxes where they would chew on hay for the next few hours. They were the kind of people who would wait, standing in the cold for as long as it took to get something for practically nothing. Knight would have his work cut out.

Ernie showed up, shambling down the road. The same age, we had both quit school at the same time and had hung around together ever since, seldom doing anything useful, anything that paid a dollar that is. There weren't that many jobs to be had, so we just hung around, playing a little shinny hockey, going to auction sales and anything else to kill the dark winter days and evenings.

"Hey, Ern. How about giving me a hand with the stoves?"

"What are you paying? You know I don't work for nothing," he said with a lopsided grin on his thin face. "You dumb bugger, you've probably got a roaring fire going in them and I'll burn my new mitts."

"Naw, they should be cold by now," I said. "I thought maybe a couple of old ladies would come by and help me, but you'll have to do."

We went inside where Olwyn was sweeping.

"Now be careful when you pull those pipes apart," she said, "I'm trying to clean up in here."

"Yeah . . . we'll be careful. Aughhh, hell! Look at that! Sorry . . ." Ernie's usual grin faded as the soot came cascading from the disjointed pipe that he had dislodged with a swipe of his mittened hand.

"Never mind, we'll clean it up as soon as we get the stoves out of the way."

The kitchen stove was a heavy old clunker. Gurney Oxford, the lettering on the oven door said. Its peeling chrome and multiple dents testified to its age. A couple of farmers, seeing us struggling with it, grabbed hold, and we got it through the door. It sat there in the frozen yard, canted at an angle, a pile of rusted metal. The heart of our home for as long as I could remember, it looked like it had suffered cardiac arrest. Again I wondered who would want an old stove like that.

The bidding started. Knight's mellifluent baritone gaining power as it warmed to the task. He started with small things—fruit canning jars, buckets, curtains—things that occupied space on larger pieces.

"What'my bid for these good Mason jars, not a cracked one in the lot. Who'll start it?"

"Five cents." Almost inaudible, the timorous bid came from the middle of the throng.

I had packed the jars, a dozen to a box, expecting Art to sell them by the box, but no, he drew them out separately. He knew that the bidding would start at ten cents for a full box, and he might work it up to a quarter. Individually they would bring, perhaps, ten cents apiece. It meant that he would work harder, but the end result was more money in the till—and in his pocket. That's why he was in demand as an auctioneer; he knew his crowd, and he worked it to the limit.

With Ernie helping, I kept moving things forward as Knight indicated what he wanted next. He pointed at the washing machine. Between us we carried it, set it down in front of him, and opened the lid to expose the inner workings. He went into a long chant without eliciting any response. They stood, wooden faced, shuffling slightly, but not looking at anything in particular. Here's one thing I guess we're stuck with, I thought. Knight's voice was running down. Like a spring-wound gramophone, it was losing momentum. I was about to move the sad old appliance out of the way when from somewhere in the middle of that silent crowd, a clear voice announced.

"Five dollars!"

There was dead silence as for a few seconds everyone froze, and then heads turned, seeking the source of such an audacious bid. Even the auctioneer went silent, his mouth hanging slack.

It was a woman's voice, a most unusual sound. Men's were the only voices raised at auction sales. There were a few wives, but mostly they kept quiet, relying on their menfolk to bid on some coveted item once sufficient feminine pressure had been exerted to make them do so.

"Did I hear five dollars . . . is that right . . . five dollars I'm bid?" Knight had found his voice and located the source of the offer.

"Yes, that's right. I bid five dollars." The woman stepped forward. A young woman, slight as a bird, barely five feet tall. She was neat as a pin and shining clean from the top of her black karakul hat that covered all but a few wisps of curling blonde hair, down her thigh-length sheepskin coat to a pair of slim blue-jean clad legs that ended in tooled leather riding boots. I had never seen her before, nor had I ever seen a woman wearing blue jeans before. Most of those standing there hadn't either by their startled expressions and whispered comments. She had a confident air about her, though, a confidence that said she didn't give a damn what they thought. She showed impatience at Knight's hesitation. She expected her bid to be accepted without further nonsense. Knight made a token gesture, but he knew it would be a miracle if someone improved on it.

"I have five, who'll give me five and a quarter?" he chanted. He might as well have saved his voice.

"Sold!" His hammer came down on our kitchen table, with a thump. "Sold to . . . What is your name, Ma'am?"

"Just mark it down as Helen. I'll pay you right now, and if someone will help me load it, I'll get it out of your way." She opened her purse and extracted a five-dollar bill. She handed it to the clerk who stared at it for a moment, holding it stretched tight between his hands, before depositing with the quarters and fifty-cent pieces in his cash box.

She worked her way out back, but in a few minutes

reappeared sitting on the seat of a light sleigh drawn by a spanking team of chestnuts, their coats glistening and their harness oiled and ornamented. The crowd parted, letting her through, and half a dozen farmers fell all over themselves to help load that old washing machine and tie it down. Then with a click of her tongue and a shake of the reins, she was gone with most of us looking after her. Who was she? I never found out.

I began looking for more small things to bring forward, things I had brought outside but seemed to have vanished, things I knew hadn't been sold. Out of the corner of my eye, I saw Ray McCormick walking up the road, our kerosene lantern and our bucksaw in his hands.

"Hey Ray!" I called, "where are you going with that stuff."

"I'm going home with it. That's where. Why?"

"How come you're just taking it. Why don't you buy it?"

"I just did."

"Yeah, from who and for how much?"

"From that kid brother of yours. He's selling all kinds of stuff down there in the garage. I paid him three dollars for this junk."

"My brother! You got to be kidding. He's in school."

"You want to bet? You go down there and have a look. He's got a regular store going."

Ray was right. Owen wasn't in school. He was down there in our garage with his own sale going on and, by all appearances, he was doing as well as Art Knight. He had gathered up a bunch of small stuff: tools, books, old car parts . . . whatever he could spirit away. Some of it, I was sure, I had never seen before. The strange thing was people were buying it. He had quite a crowd in there.

He looked at me, half guilty, half daring me to say anything. What the hell, I thought, he's making as much as Knight is. I went back to helping.

The sun came out, warming the backs of those still standing around visiting. The yard had emptied of items to sell and of people to buy them. The rigs were heading home with things that had been part of my life sticking out of sleigh boxes. The sale was about over. Knight and his clerk were conferring over the cash box.

There was not much left, even things I thought wouldn't sell were gone. The rest would go to the dump. I wondered about the kitchen stove, still sitting there, its legs gradually sinking into the thawing ground. How am I going to get rid of that?

"Hey! I gonna take dat stove off your hands for you. You don't gonna need it no more."

I turned. The voice belonged to a short grimy individual with a moth-eaten fur hat screwed around on his head so that one earflap partially covered one eye. John Otterwerker. He had been one of the first to come and, as far as I could remember, he hadn't bought anything.

"It ought to be worth something," I said.

"What an old stove like dat gonna be wort. I gonna get wit it for you."

"How about fifty cents."

"Feefty cents! I got no feefty cents. I got feefty cents, I gonna buy someting. I got no feefty cents."

I was about to say "OK, take it," when Owen walked over.

"Hey, Rudy Eichorn wants to buy the stove. He said he'd give me a dollar for it."

I glanced at Otterwerker. He looked startled.

"He gonna give you a dollar for dat old stove. He mebbe reech, or crazy, or someting?"

Owen kind of grinned.

"Yep, that's what he said. He'd give me a dollar."

"Dat old stove she's not wort no dollar." He nudged it with his toe. "Where dat Eichorn? He not here."

"He's gone to get his sleigh," said Owen.

"He not here, he not coming back." Otterwerker glanced up the road where Eichorn's team would appear.

"He'll be back," said Owen.

"He don't need dat old stove. I need it dat. I gonna give you sewnty-five cents for dat. He not coming back."

I looked at Owen. He had a glint in his eye.

"I can square it with Rudy. If you really want it that bad, you can have it for seventy-five cents, but you better move it before he gets here."

Otterwerker reached in his pocket and pulled out a fat roll of bills, peeled off a dollar and handed it to Owen.

"I need it twenny-five cents."

We looked at each other and then at that roll of bills. That cagey old bugger wasn't as broke as he let on. And here I was feeling sorry for him. Owen handed him a quarter and we all grabbed on and humped the stove across the road and into Otterwerker's sleigh.

As we walked back toward the house, I said to Owen, "Do you think Eichorn's going to be mad?"

"Rudy? . . . nah . . . He never offered me no dollar. I never even saw him. I just wasn't going to let old Otterwerker get that stove for nothing. That's all." He grinned.

We went back inside. It was cold in that vacant shell of a house. It was no longer our home. All sense of 'our place' was gone from it. Olwyn was still cleaning up. She had her coat on and a beret aslant on her head.

"What are you two looking so pleased about?"

"Nothing," I said.

"We're just glad the sale is over and you can all go to the coast," Owen said. "I'm staying." He grinned. "I've got nine dollars and eighty cents. That ought to keep me going for awhile."

We wandered from room to room. It was an eerie dead place with just the smells and the marks on the walls and floors left to say we had ever lived here. Through the window I saw Art Knight's sedan pull away from in front and then the door opened and Father came in. He was jovial, excessively so, and the smell of beer was strong on him. After a few minutes, I asked, "Did we make any money?"

His face darkened.

"That, young man, is none of your business."

I didn't really care, as long as he paid my way to the Coast. At the Coast there was work and wages for doing it. I shrugged and Owen and I went outside. Olwyn followed leaving him standing alone in the empty house.

It was ten to nine; the train was due any time. I hadn't slept well. Owen and I had ranged the town until pretty late saying goodbye and then I had wound up at Ernie's house and we had talked half the night away. I would miss Ernie, but he would be the only one. Mother, Father, Owen and I had rooms at the hotel. Olwyn had slept at Stickles'. We were on the platform waiting for the train, when I noticed Owen was missing. I hadn't seen him leave. Bruce Merryweather came by the station.

"Have you seen Owen," I asked.

"No, but I bet he's up at the school."

"At the school, what would he be doing there?"

"I don't know, but I bet that's where he is."

That stupid kid, I thought as I took off on the run.

Owen was at the school. He was in a huddle with a few of his buddies. They were horsing around, as usual. I grabbed him by the arm.

"C'mon, stupid. The train's coming."

"Yeah, Yeah . . . Let it come."

I hauled on him. The school bell rang, and at the same time the train whistle blew at the edge of town. Everybody headed for the school door. Owen moved as if to follow them.

"C'mon," I said, "let's go. We'll miss the train."

He sort of waved at the retreating backs. Nobody saw; they were filing into the school.

"Yeah . . . I guess so." A tear slid down his face, and his mouth trembled slightly: "Stinking coast."

We broke into a run.

Afterword

THE EVENTS IN THIS BOOK ARE ALL TRUE. THEY HAPPENED PRETTY much as I have recounted them. They did, though, take place a long time ago, and memory is fallible. For that reason, I do not pretend that this is a verbatim account.

The people are also real people, tough resilient people, many of whom had a hand in shaping my life and the lives of my sister and brother as we grew into adulthood. I have no wish to show any of them in a bad light. Therefore, wherever there seemed a chance, however remote, of that happening, I concealed them behind fictitious names.

If I have cast an unkind shadow upon anyone mentioned in these pages, or any of their descendants, I am truly sorry. It was not my intention to do so.

Index

235

PRINTED AND BOUND
IN BOUCHERVILLE, QUÉBEC, CANADA
BY MARC VEILLEUX IMPRIMEUR INC.
IN OCTOBER, 1998